Royal Highlander

Royal Highlander

A Soldier of H. M. 42nd (Royal)
Highlanders During the Peninsular,
South of France and Waterloo
Campaigns of the Napoleonic Wars

James Anton

LEONAUR

Royal Highlander: A Soldier of H. M. 42nd (Royal)
Highlanders During the Peninsular, South of France
and Waterloo Campaigns of the Napoleonic Wars
by James Anton

Published by Leonaur Ltd

Originally published in 1841 under the title
Retrospect of a Military Life

ISBN: 978-1-84677-223-8 (hardcover)
ISBN: 978-1-84677-224-5 (softcover)

http://www.leonaur.com

Publisher's Note

The opinions expressed in this book are those of the author
and are not necessarily those of the publisher.

Contents

Publisher's Note

The original edition of James Anton's memoir, published in 1841 continued beyond the end of the present volume to tell of his further service on garrison duty in Gibraltar and Ireland and of his conversion to the Protestant faith. Unlike the author's accounts of his adventures in the Napoleonic Wars this material is of little interest, other than to social historians perhaps; it tells primarily of the army's role in dealing with civil unrest, and for this reason we have taken the liberty of excising the final few chapters.

We would suggest that Anton himself may have initially set out to write a memoir devoted solely to his exploits in the Napoleonic Wars—and nothing else. The passages that appear in this book as the author's afterword were, in the text as first published, the concluding paragraphs of Chapter 15 (Chapter 15 in our volume also). Anton's words suggest to us that he believed he had reached the end of his narrative, he decided, however, to write on.

We believe that the changes we have made have resulted in a stronger and more relevant edition of one of the most colourful Napoleonic memoirs by a highland soldier. We hope you agree!

The Leonaur Editors

CHAPTER 1

I Enlist in the Militia

The narratives of travellers frequently furnish materials for the pen of the historian, the biographer, and the novelist; and however humble the individual may be, who assumes the task of giving to the public his remarks on the passing events of his time, or the incidents that have come under his observation, he may yet be found to merit the commendation of being, at least in some degree, both interesting and useful.

Since so many military memoirs have issued from the press during the last twenty-five years, it may be thought a rather presumptive undertaking on the part of a soldier to usher another work of this kind into public notice. Yet amidst all the failures we daily witness in the book-making world, we still see fresh adventurers succeed to fill up the chasm occasioned by the unsuccessful speculations of their predecessors; and, although friendly hints may be given that this or that pursuit is overdone, the adventurers still pursue their course, and the usual results follow. Misfortune overwhelms the many, fortune favours the few, and the latter gives a stimulus to fresh adventure, while the former seldom serves as a warning to guard against the risk. That fortune has not favoured with wealth any of my *grade* of military journalists, I am aware, and the writers of this class have not been few; yet the records of some will be perused with interest, long after other wars, other enterprises, and other adventures enable other journalists to emulate, if not to excel them. With this prospect before me, I venture to incur the risk.

Stimulated more by a desire to merit the esteem of my friends, and the good opinion of all who wish to maintain strict discipline in the army, than to reap any substantial reward for the labour of my pen, I come forward to offer this my mite for the use of those who may be pleased to cater for the public information, and lay before them some incidents which may have escaped the observation of more distinguished writers. With respect to the merits of the performance, I must leave it to the discrimination of the reader, either to censure my presumption, despise my folly, or allow both to pass off disregarded. If censure be awarded, and the work condemned, I shall have this gratification—however mortifying it may be to my feelings to be censured, I involve no one in the loss but myself.

I shall not weary my reader by a recital of the uninteresting occurrences of my boyish days, but pass on to the period when I was about to bid farewell to my friends and native village.

It was in the winter of 1802 that the Militia were about to be enrolled, and as my inclination was bent upon the army, I considered this the time to offer my service, if it would be accepted; but I dreaded much being rejected, as I had been, on a former occasion, for the Line, in consequence of my boyish appearance and low stature. I succeeded, however, on half *tiptoe.*, to strike the gauge, and was sworn in, a happy little fellow. Happy indeed, for the inseparable companion of my youth, my earliest acquaintance and friend, had been enrolled that day for the same corps; and I should have been grievously disappointed at being separated from him.

I cannot say, however, that this happiness was altogether unmixed with grief, particularly when I was about to take farewell of my poor widowed mother, whose heart was like to break at what, to say the least of it, she considered a very foolish step of her son, and likely to lead to the ruin not only of his soul but of his body also. But, perhaps, few mothers feel otherwise than sorrowful at parting with their children, when about to enter upon a career so little in unison with the peaceful habits of a country or village life. Having blessed me in all the sincerity of a mother's heart, she recommended me to my friend, as if he had been a sage of fourscore years. Huntly, for that is the name by which I shall have occasion to mention my friend in the course of my narrative, promised to conform in all she solicited; and I must do him the justice to say, he never failed in that promise, so far as circumstances permitted.

Huntly was, like myself, the son of a poor widow, who, in order to gain an honest livelihood, on the death of her husband, took up a school for the education of children; and, if I mistake not, it was the only one in the village kept by a female, for the purpose of teaching girls to knit as well as read. She might, indeed, have been considered more as a nurse to the children than a useful teacher of the English language, for they were placed under her care at so early an age, that she had frequently to take one on her knee and point out to it the letters of the alphabet, before it could well pronounce the name. I have often observed her seated in this manner, explaining the forms of this and that letter, in order to draw from the child the name, but to no effect, for the infant had fallen asleep in her arms. Had a parent been present to observe her on occasions of this kind, it could not have failed to excite a very favourable opinion of the widow. How tenderly she raised up the sleeper, and with a threatening nod, directed towards some noisy urchins, softened every voice to a whisper, until she had placed her sleeping charge on her bed, where it reposed as if under the eye of its mother. Her manner of teaching was just that which was best adapted for curbing in children that passionate excitement which bad nurses too frequently encourage in the infant mind. When any of the children chanced to stumble or fall, she would, instead of exciting its anger against the inanimate object that had occasioned the accident, in an instant soothe its sudden sorrow and its cries by assuring the infant that she would forgive it, at that time, for injuring the object which had been in its way; and thus, instead of exciting the child's passion, she never failed in drawing forth its sympathy, and in convincing it that itself had been the offender.

The widow was certainly well respected in the village, and, though poor, I have heard her frequently boast, when advising Huntly, that she had been enabled to bring him up without incurring a debt that she was unable to discharge, save that which she owed to her Creator, and that she hoped he would always preserve the same spirit of uprightness and independence, and submit to every privation rather than forfeit the name of an honest man. Hopes had been frequently held out to her, that were she to conform to the established church, she might be recommended for a small salary, for she was a very useful woman in the place, but she preferred her own nonconforming principles to all the wealth that could be held out to induce her to abandon them. Yet, notwithstanding this rigidness, she would not suffer a child under her care to be instructed otherwise than agreeably to the doctrine of the national church. The Assembly's Catechism was the first book put into the hands of a child; the Proverbs of Solomon, the New Testament, and the Bible, were the successive class-books in the widow's infant school. The latter book limited the extent of Huntly's education, with a little smattering of writing and the three first rules of arithmetic. With regard to grammar, he knew as little of it as I did myself, and that did not enable me to distinguish a *noun* from a *verb,* or an *article* from a *preposition.*

Huntly's father had left, at his death, a tenement of ground and a few dilapidated houses, together with about an acre of land contiguous: the annual rent and *feu* duty paid for the whole amounted only to a few shillings. This, with the infant school and her abstemious manner of living, enabled the widow to rear up her children in a decent respectable manner, if compared with some of those of the neighbourhood. She had placed Huntly with a weaver, who rented a shop under her own roof, to learn the weaving business; he was not satisfied with the choice made for him; and whether through a desire of seeing a little more of the world, or getting quit of a sedentary employment, it is needless to inquire; he emancipated himself from one service and bound himself to another.

It was in April 1803 that my friend and I, accompanied by a number of young men, enrolled for the militia, and left our native village, proud of being considered soldiers.

Having bidden farewell to our friends, we proceeded on our journey, which eventually has proved a long one, not yet finished, having been occasionally protracted by casual sojourns, and lengthened out by frequent demands on our service, the particulars of which I intend to place before my readers. In the mean time, I do not hold out to their expectation a tale of misery, of misfortune, of oppression, or of unmerited sufferings. Thank God, we yet serve, and are, comparatively speaking, happy, notwithstanding the lapse of so many years; we have gradually advanced, never retrograded, and are possessed of a competent share of our provident savings (not the fruits of guilty plunderings, with which our hands were never stained), to enable us, with our expected pension, to enjoy the comforts of civil life, when our military service is over.

We arrived at Aberdeen, received our billets, and the following day commenced our military avocations.

At that time trade was unusually brisk, and improvements were in progress in every direction round that city: extensive manufactories had been established, were now enlarging, and others were forming; new streets were opening in various directions; large handsome buildings were advancing on every side; a splendid house for the office of the Aberdeen Banking Company was nearly finished, and a new bridge was in great forwardness over the Den burn. These, with the erection of a number of small cottages along the banks of the canal and avenues leading to the city, gave such an active appearance to the scene, that I have not witnessed the like since. Certainly, the prospect was considerably enhanced in my estimation, by its being then altogether new to me. Yet, on the whole, there certainly was something more interesting about the city and its environs at that time than perhaps may be witnessed for centuries afterwards. In short, I thought Aberdeen the focus of the happiest circle in the world; all was stirring life, nothing but cheerful bustle and business, while the youth from the farthest bounds of the Highland districts were pouring in for the purpose of being trained to arms.

We had been only a few days in billet-quarters, when we were ordered to occupy the barracks. Here my pay-sergeant made choice of me to serve one of the officers. I was quite elated at being thus selected; however, my sergeant, to make sure of my abilities, gave me a pair of his own shoes to clean, as a trial; this I finished so much in my own old country fashion, that he deemed me unfit for the situation.

I should not be doing justice, however, to that worthy non-commissioned officer, who is now in his grave, in neglecting to mention that he pointed out one of the men, who had seen some service, to show me how to clean my own shoes and appointments. For this mark of attention to me, I acknowledged myself obliged to the sergeant, as well as to the man who had been so good as condescend to do me this service. Perhaps there was something of unsoldierlike awkwardness, or silly simplicity, in the manner in which I expressed my thanks, that drew upon me the sarcastic sneer of a little old snuffy snivelling soldier, named David Duffus, who was standing rubbing his breastplate beside the sergeant.

"Ha!" he exclaimed, addressing himself to the man who had been instructing me; "he'll make an excellent soldier that; he's a fine smooth-faced, soft-tongued, simple, ignorant boy."

This remark was made more with the intention of showing off his knowledge of character, than out of any desire to hurt my pride; and I joined with the rest in the smile at my own simplicity and ignorance.

It may be a matter of doubt, whether learning or unlettered

ignorance enables a private soldier the better to submit with cheerfulness to all the commands which duty and discipline exact. Learning, when ill-directed, becomes a curse to him, for he is considered the stimulator of others to disobedience, by becoming an advocate in their cause; and when found in a fault, his knowledge adds to its weight, and magnifies it to a crime, in the military code; while in the ignorant defaulter, some redeeming qualification will plead in palliation of the offence. Learning, unpromoted, is frequently if not always grumbling, and by this means prevents itself from meriting reward. The ignorant man remains contented because he knows himself incapable of performing the duties annexed to the higher ranks; he knows also that the door of preferment is not entirely shut against him, if by his own exertions he strives to merit distinction. The knowledge of this is wisdom in the unlettered man; the lack of this knowledge is folly as well as ignorance in the man of education.

I do not know a more miserable being in the army than the self-sufficient arrogant man, who considers himself "all-wise" and "all-knowing." He lectures to others concerning their ignorance and folly, while he himself becomes the dupe of those whom he considers less knowing, yet who take the advantage of him, and leave him in the lurch, with his pretended wisdom for his consolation.

I have been led to make these observations, in consequence of the misadventures of the man who made the foregoing remark on myself. He had received a tolerably good education, and had in early life been an itinerant dancing-master. Dissatisfied with that way of life, he enlisted in a Fencible regiment stationed in Ireland, where he served some years. Having been discharged at the close of the war, he entered as a substitute to serve in the militia. He was considered a *knowing one;* his taste for dancing led him to frequent *jig-houses,* when he should have been in his barrack; and, after repeated warnings, he was brought to the halberds; soon after which he deserted, and was not heard of afterwards.

I had gone through my *facings* very easily, and was, after a fortnight's drill, honoured with a firelock. My pay-sergeant was the drill of the squad in which I was placed, and I was getting on, I thought, very fast, and was very proud of the sergeant's praise. However, on one unlucky morning, my right-hand comrade sportingly whispered to me, as we brought our pieces to the level, at the word of command, *present:*

"I ha'e *Cocky Ross* i' my e'e."

"*Sheet* him, then," I whispered back.

The sergeant could not overhear us, being more than twenty paces off, and our intentions were perfectly harmless, as we had wooden drivers in our firelocks, and no ammunition in our possession. But those senseless whispers excited laughter, to which I was very prone, and my comrades joined in the smirk. For this ill-timed laugh, five of us were committed to the guard-house, with a threat of having us tried by a court-martial; and at the time in question very little constituted a crime sufficient for that purpose: we got off, however, with two nights' confinement; and from that day I never attempted *to* laugh or make sport in the ranks.

A regiment, on its being embodied, is generally submitted to more rigid discipline than one of many years' standing; the *materiel* of which it is composed renders this absolutely necessary.

Here in our lower ranks are to be found men of sober, quiet, obedient dispositions; others, drunken, turbulent, disaffected, and disorderly, whom nothing but the strong arm of the law and coercive measures will keep in any degree of subordination, and prevent from domineering over their peaceable well-disposed comrades; and it is only the disaffected, the licentious, and ill-disposed, that consider the prompt enforcement of order and discipline, by coercive measures, dispensable or unnecessary in the army.

Philanthropists, who decry the lash, ought to consider in what manner the good men—the deserving, exemplary soldiers—are to be protected; if no coercive measures are to be resorted to on purpose to prevent ruthless ruffians from insulting with impunity the temperate, the well-inclined, and the orderly-disposed, the good must be left to the mercy of the worthless; and I am glad to say there are many good men in the ranks of the army.

In civil society, the mechanic, the labourer, yea even the pauper, can remove from his dwelling or place of abode, if he finds himself annoyed by a violent or troublesome neighbour; but the good soldier cannot remove without this despicable demon of discord accompanying him, and yet we must be told that the lash is not to be used. The good soldier thanks you not for such philanthropy; the incorrigible laughs at your humanity, despises your clemency, and meditates only how to gratify his naturally vicious propensities.

I trust the reader will not think I mean to insinuate that the ranks of the army are principally composed of such characters as I here point out as incorrigible. No! the incorrigible arc few indeed, but the troublesome man has a wonderful dexterity in being present where he is not wanted, and absent where he should be present.

CHAPTER 2

I Leave My Native Land

It was not supposed, at the time of our enrolment, to be the intention of Government to keep the Militia regiments embodied beyond twenty-eight days annually; but during that short period, war was declared, or anticipated, and we remained, contrary to expectation, to follow a military life.

In the month of June, we were ordered to Fort-George, where we arrived after a very pleasant march by Old Meldrum, Turriff, Banff, Portsoy, Cullen, and Fochabers. In the neighbourhood of the last mentioned town is the princely residence of the Duke of Gordon. Here we were liberally entertained at the expense of his Grace, and free admission was given to view the gardens, woods, and walks around the wide domain of Gordon-Castle.

From Fochabers we proceeded by Elgin, Forres, and Nairn to the Fort.

Fort George is so remotely situated that few soldiers like to be quartered within its walls. There is no town of consequence nearer to it than Inverness, which is upwards of thirteen miles distant; and instead of bread being served out to the troops as at other stations, a certain allowance of oatmeal was issued. To our north country men, this substitute proved more acceptable than bread, as it enabled those who were inclined for a breakfast mess to have one in the manner to which they had been accustomed; to others it afforded sufficiency for cakes as well as a little surplus for sale, and a good price was received for such as we had to dispose of. We were served out with half a pound of beef or mutton per man, daily. This was a quarter of a pound less than military allowance; but if we did not get it, we did not pay for it; and we were all satisfied with the quantity, for it was fully sufficient. Indeed small allowances of provisions are always best, when we can purchase to our own satisfaction either with regard to quantity or quality. Why force upon us more than is barely necessary for subsistence, when we can get of our own choice to purchase? The quarter-masters will not bear me out in this, but the soldiers will. The former will say, "The men will get drunk if they get money;" the latter may with as much justice say, "Gluttony is worse than drunkenness."

The country, in approaching the Fort, is a bare, bleak, barren moor, with a few patches of ill cultivated ground, surrounding turf-built huts, which are in danger of being cast over the sterile fields like so much manure, by the wintry tempests that sweep over that unsheltered wild. The Moray Firth washes three sides of the Fort, and on the other, the irreclaimable face of the country scarcely produces a blade of grass; furze bushes are thinly sprinkled over the rough stony moor, for upwards of a mile, in the direction of the small village of Campbeltown; but even to that place, inconsiderable as it was, we were not permitted to go, as it was beyond the prescribed limits. On purpose to evade this inhibition, some soldiers, of a regiment quartered in the Fort, lifted the milestone and placed it against the further end of the public-house in which they intended to regale themselves, and when they were brought back, and about to be tried for surpassing the limits prescribed for their perambulations, they pleaded that they had not gone beyond the milestone, and were pardoned; no doubt, more on account of the humour of the frolic than of the right to legal exculpation.

Notwithstanding these circumscribed bounds, to which I may say we were confined, the Fort afforded pleasures enough for me; my wants were few and easily gratified; if I was inclined for exercise, the drill-ground afforded ample space for any gymnastic amusement, and there were never wanting some congenial spirits to enter the lists. If I wished to indulge myself in solitude, I could do so without interruption, and, though the neighbourhood presented little but sterility, the distant prospect was interesting and grand. Methinks I even now cast my eyes towards the mountains and shores of Ross, where ancient Channery and pleasant Rosemarknie display their busy craft along the shelving coast. The setting sun imbeds himself in golden skirted clouds, and throws his amber beams over the waters, to the dark woods of Culloden; while the shadows of a hundred hills extend over the placid Firth, and rise on the bristled bastions of the garrison.

But the low man of sensuality loves the house of debauchery better than the contemplation of such prospects as these; his licentious spirit finds no pleasure but in scenes of intemperance and riot, which inevitably lead him to infamy and disgrace.

Indeed, I look back to Fort George as the place where I first enjoyed freedom, and to the time of my residence there as the beginning of the enjoyment of life. I was then astonished to hear men complaining of want of amusement, and want of luxuries, to which they had been accustomed. Perhaps the manner in which I had been brought up tended to promote this feeling of satisfaction which I enjoyed. I had been habituated to the most simple and spare diet upon which youth could subsist, while at the same time my mother never failed to impress upon me the praiseworthy qualifications of temperance, industry, and economy. Indeed, Sparta never had her equal in respect to what may be called self-denial; and she ceased not, by precept as well as example, to impress upon me the same contempt of ease and luxury which she herself entertained.

After being brought up in this manner, I can feel no surprise at my being then better satisfied with my lot than those who had been more indulged; and that life which thousands looked upon as bondage, I considered freedom, and was seldom or never unhappy.

Indeed, of all the ranks in the army, none has so little to give his mind uneasiness as the private soldier. He is answerable only for his own conduct, while every other rank, from the corporal up to the general, feels an anxiety respecting the duty and conduct of those under him, in as much as he may incur censure for their neglect of duty, or for an overstretch of authority on his own part; and though the blame and punishment may fall heavier on those who have been personally guilty, yet there is in the army a certain responsibility on the superior which gives him no cause to exonerate himself when any failure in those under him takes place; consequently, he must be always on the alert to guard against crime or neglect, and cannot enjoy that independent ease of mind which a private soldier may do; yet, notwithstanding the enviable ease of mind within reach of the latter, it would not answer the purposes of the army were every man to remain satisfied with his lowly rank, as it is essentially necessary that soldiers should be possessed of ambition; their country demands it, and ease of mind must be sacrificed to the necessities of duty, however poor the reward.

The regiment remained in Fort George until the end of October, when we proceeded on our route to Edinburgh.

The weather was rather unfavourable during our march, but the kindly manner in which we were generally received by those on whom we were billeted, made us forget the unpleasant weather and disregard our fatigues. Better would it be for some soldiers, when on the line of inarch, were they to make themselves satisfied with, and agreeable to, those on whom they may be billeted, and refrain from insisting on having accommodation to which they have a doubtful claim. I have been frequently received in a rather ungracious manner, but invariably found some kindly attention paid to me before parting.

It is often the case in Scotland and Ireland, that soldiers are quartered on a class of people who have so little accommodation for their own families, that they cannot look with any degree of complacency on the poor wearied soldier, when he enters their house; but this is only the impulse of a moment, and a more kindly feeling will be found to succeed this momentary displeasure, when no insolence is offered to cause its continuance. I have frequently seen the mistress pf the house, on which I have been billeted, under the necessity of making a bed of straw for some of her own family, in order to afford a bed for myself and comrade; but this I rejected, and requested permission to lie on the straw. I have seen some soldiers, however, insist on having the second best bed in the house, provided there were a choice to be had, and even telling the landlord or landlady that a soldier had a right to the best. Such conduct is detestable.

Our route was directed by Nairn, Forres, and Elgin. At the latter place, the ruins of the old cathedral continue to attract the attention of strangers and the lovers of antiquity.

From Elgin we proceeded to Fochabers, thence to Huntly, by Keith. There are two towns of this name, the old and the new. The former, situated on the Isla, is of great antiquity, but now dwindled to a few houses. On the north bank of the river, and overlooking the bridge, is the house of Cooperhill; this has been a public-house from time immemorial, and is memorable in the neighbourhood for having been taken possession of by a band of outlaws, who were set upon plundering the country, but were defeated here with great loss. The defeat was principally owing to the presence of mind of the maid-servant, who was employed in preparing *sowens* before the door of the house when the *Cateran* or *banditti* approached. They were led on by Petrie Roy, a daring Highlander, who, the better to secure the attachment of his followers, gave out that no man born of woman could vanquish him. This, he alleged, had been announced to him by a familiar spirit, or *weird*. He had been successful in levying contributions on the

22

low country, and had carried off an immense number of cattle to the Highlands. Strengthened by fresh adventurers, and encouraged by the mysterious being with whom he was supposed to have intercourse, and who had announced in her own enigmatical manner, on being consulted by him, previous to his setting out on this adventure, "Hold on to Keith, and then to Leith;" full of the hopes that he should plunder successfully all the way, he arrived at Cooperhill about breakfast-time; and as no such guests were expected, no preparations had been made. The country was not yet alarmed, nor apprehensive of receiving such unwelcome visitors. The *Cateran* (for such those robbers were designated as a body) placed their muskets against the wall of the house, and set about enjoying themselves at free quarters within. Meantime the servant-maid very dexterously contrived to pour a small quantity of sowens into each of the muskets*, without being observed, and messengers were despatched to alarm the country; while the bellman, perched in a window under the kirk-bell, began to sound the tocsin, and it is said that the knells were heard throughout the neighbouring parish of Grange to a distance of eight miles.

The country assembled from all sides, rallying under the banner of Glengarrick. The Highlanders issued forth tumultuously on the first sound of alarm, seized their arms, and urged on by their leader and animated by the loud warlike notes of the bagpipe, flew to the kirk in order to seize the ringer; but he was perched above their reach, their muskets were found to be useless, and he continued his powerful exertions until the bell rent.

The inhabitants were assembling fast, and the conflict, the details of which are now involved in some doubt, was commenced either in the churchyard, or on the bridge over the Isla. According to the traditional parochial accounts, Glengarrick was the hero, a strong powerful man, the owner of some

---

*From this circumstance arose the by-word, common in the north of Scotland, when a piece misses fire, *there is sowens in your gun.*

lands on the banks of Isla, now known by the name of New-mills. His mother died before giving him birth, and he was extracted by the Caesarean operation. So far the legendary accounts affirm, in order perhaps to accomplish him for the overthrow of his weirded antagonist.

Glengarrick's first fury lighted on the piper, whom he threw over the bridge into the Isla, which bore him down its rapid stream to the *linn** (or fall), over which he was pre-cipitated, still firmly grasping his pipes, which gave their last groan as their owner sunk in the agitated waters below.

Having despatched the man of martial music, Glengarrick next encountered the chief himself. The conflict would have been worthy of a place in the Iliad, had the two chiefs fought under the Trojan wall, and had had a Homer to record the contest; but under the walls of a poor obscure parish-kirk, and among the silent dwellings of the dead, no record perpetu-ates the event, no bard has given the song of exultation to the victor, or of lamentation for the vanquished, to awaken the remembrance of the strife among future generations. Petrie, pressed hard by the powerful arm of Glengarrick, began to parley, at the same time acquainting the latter that no man born of woman could overcome him.

"Then I am that man!" exclaimed the fresh-inspired chief, "and your days are numbered."

The Highlander recoiled a pace, his heel struck a half-sunk gravestone, he fell backwards, and was pierced under the ribs by the victor. Meantime the Cateran, finding their muskets useless, threw them aside, and engaged hand to hand with their increasing and implacable enemies: they flew to the as-sistance of their fallen chief, and Glengarrick would have been included among the number of the slain, had not a blacksmith (not inferior to the one who fought against Clan Quhele on the North Inch of Perth) sprung to his assistance, armed with one of the biers (hand-spokes) on which the dead are borne

*The *linn* is nearly a mile from the bridge.

to the grave, and with his own hand laid twelve of the outlaws lifeless at his feet. The sun was set before the few surviving Highlanders fled from the scene of strife, leaving their helpless companions to the mercy of their victors, and their dead to find a grave beneath a *cairn*.

Petrie, neglected amidst the excited combatants, withdrew to a neighbouring farm, and took shelter in a barn, where, faint and exhausted, he sunk down on a heap of straw. Here he was discovered by a young woman belonging to the house. Surprised at the strange appearance of the blood-besprinkled man stretched before her, she flew to her master, lately returned from the fight, and related to him the discovery she had made. The outlaw was immediately secured and conveyed from Keith to Leith, where it is said he died of his wounds.

The new town of Keith is about a mile from the old town, and was begun to be built in 1750, on a barren heathy moor, the property of the Earl of Findlater. It consists of three broad streets, with several others crossing, all of them in straight lines; and there is a spacious square in the centre, which forms the market-place.

Notwithstanding the original sterility of the ground on which the village has been erected, by the encouragement of the proprietor, and the industry of the settlers, the soil has amply rewarded the labourer for his toil, and recompensed the proprietor for the encouragement given, by increasing the value of his adjacent lands.

About two miles from Keith is the village of New-mills; it is the property of the Earl of Fife, and was *feued* for building about twenty years after the former. It is more pleasantly situated, having the Isla running close by it; several bleachfields line the banks of the river, and the whole site is also reclaimed from a barren waste; cultivation is spreading rapidly around, and bidding fair to banish the dreary solitudes of Aultmore.

The first *feuars* of this village were poor emigrants from the remote glens of the Highland districts; being hemmed in on every side by wealthy neighbours, who proscribed their little flocks from trespassing on pastures once considered free, but now fanned and rented by strangers, no alternative was left but to perish in poverty or remove. Here they found an asylum; here they struggled with adversity, and, persevering, overcame it by industry. The children now have the pleasant prospect of green fields, fruit-trees, and rich crops, where their fathers, at their settlement, saw only the yellow furze, the hardy juniper, the fern, or the stunted heath.

From Keith we climb the dark brow of the Balloch and approach Huntly.

Huntly! Oh, how sweet is that name to my ear! Thirty years have nearly elapsed since the period of which I now write, yet the prospect is fresh before me, and dear to my remembrance is each object. Methinks I approach that delightful valley, and with light elastic step sweep round the skirts of the rocky Bin, and cast my eye on the winding Deveron, as it rolls rapidly past the ruins where rest the remains of my humble ancestors. Humble, indeed; forgotten, they lie in yonder solitary neglected spot*, where the mouldering walls crumble over their graves, and the long nettle, the thistle, the dock, and the briar mingle their heads over the silent dwellings of the dead. Flow on, thou troubled stream; I love thy hoarse murmurings; perhaps my own bones may yet rest on thy green banks, if they escape withering on the battle-field of a foreign land.

I now turn my eye towards the dilapidated remains of ancient grandeur: roofless stands the castle, tenanted by noisy daws. What devastations do a few years make on the perishable works of man! Often have I climbed its lofty battlements and admired the figures carved round the caves. There, on a belt of no mean architecture, were conspicuous the founders' names—GEORGE GORDON, FIRST MARQUIS, AND HENRIETTA STEWART, FIRST MARCHIONESS OF HUNTLY—the date 1605. These are now effaced, the roof has disappeared, the stairs are gone, and the succeeding generation may perhaps say,

* The churchyard and ruins of Peterkirk.

"Where did the castle stand?" A modern building (Huntly Lodge) looks towards the ruins, and owes not a little of its aggrandizement to the dilapidation of the latter. I hail thee, Huntly, my native place, the abode of my industrious, honest, frugal friends. I appreciate all the former acts of kindness conferred on me, and I now feel proud of the welcome I receive; yet scarcely have I time to acknowledge it before I must bid adieu.

CHAPTER 3

I Join the 42nd Regiment

From Huntly we proceeded by Inverury to Aberdeen; thence by Stonehaven to Lawrencekirk. On leaving Stonehaven we crossed a small stream, which recent rains had swollen beyond its usual channel; there were stepping-stones, so that one could have easily avoided dipping his foot in the stream; but not to lose time in passing, the rear pressed forward on the front, so as to occasion a jostling, by which a number missed the stones and slipped into the water: I was one of this number, and with my shoes well soaked, and pinching my toes, marched on to Lawrencekirk. By this time my feet were blistered, my ankles swollen, and my shoulders cut with my knapsack slings.

Fortunately I got a good billet, as usual, though nearly a mile from the town. My worthy landlady, who had all the milk of human kindness in her disposition, made me sit down and bathe my feet; for I was about to go to the mill-dam for that purpose, but she would not permit me; but ordered warm water, and gave me some whisky to rub on my ankles; and this, in a few hours, had the desired effect of allaying the swelling and removing the pain. My comrades (for there were four of us in the billet) rallied and jeered me on being the *gudewife's* favourite; but I did not take these rubs amiss, and my hostess was not the less kind to me.

From Lawrencekirk we marched to Brechin, a neat town situated on the side of a hill, overlooking the richest soil, and the best cultivated I had ever seen. The South Esk, a beautiful river, flows past Brechin towards Montrose, where it falls into a bay of the German Ocean.

The cathedral church and adjoining tower are of great antiquity; the former was built in the twelfth century, the latter at an earlier period: it is a distinct building from the church, though separated only by a few inches; it is a hundred and three feet in height, and was built by the Picts.

The country about Brechin has been the scene of many contests recorded in the annals of Scotland. Between this town and Dundee lies the moor of Manroman, lately a free public common or government property. The old inhabitants remember when this moor extended more than eight miles in length by six in breadth, without the mark of a plough-share; but of late years, successive encroachments have been made upon it by the neighbouring proprietors, in making enclosures and erecting farmsteads.

The traditional accounts of old inhabitants lead us to suppose that a great battle was fought upon this spot, between the Romans and the Caledonians, before the former reached the foot of the Grampians, and in which they were defeated; and from this circumstance it received the name of Manroman, or Minroman. A number of small hillocks and long ridges are pointed out as the graves of the slain.

From Brechin we pursued our route by Forfar, Cupar-Angus, Perth, Kinross, and Queensferry, to Edinburgh; the weather continuing unfavourable, and the face of the country was frequently covered with snow.

On our arrival at Edinburgh, my comrade and I were billeted on a house in St. James' Square. The family could not, or would not, admit us, in consequence of which the servant-maid was sent with us to procure other quarters. After conducting us through countless closes and lanes, from the Calton, where she commenced her inquiries, to Blackfriars' Wynd, and from that to the Abbey, carefully selecting the most gloomy abodes of the poorest class of lodging-houses, we were settled at last, more wearied than satisfied, in an old wooden building opposite Queensberry House; and although we were made very welcome by the mistress and her family, there was something not altogether favourable in the interior management of the house; it was a promiscuous receptacle for all classes, and sometimes rather disorderly.

In a small closet adjoining that which we were to occupy, lodged three unfortunate girls, lately arrived from Hamilton, from which place they had been induced (by promises of marriage) to follow their lovers, now stationed near Edinburgh. These poor girls, after being drawn so far from home, were disappointed, and they now felt ashamed to return. Yet, although they had acted inconsiderately, and perhaps with some levity, they were neither idly nor wantonly inclined; they were diligently employed a few days *tambouring* fine muslin, and when this work failed, they rose early every morning, walked barefooted to Leith, and were there employed unshipping coals. At night they returned to a cold welcomeless house, to prepare their scanty meal; while some ungenerous hints were thrown out, as they were turned from the fire, that they might not only keep the house in fuel, but themselves above working at such a dirty job. These poor girls were sensible that they had acted wrong in leaving their home, relying on the faith of worthless lovers; but they were still honest, and as yet they had not been under the necessity of throwing themselves on the town; and the only reply given to their jeering scoffers was a sigh or a tear. They removed from that loose lodging-house, but, left to their own exertions, and more exposed to ill-advisers and bad example than to generous protectors or good company, they fell victims to their own easy belief in the word of a lover.

Loose and noisy as this lodging was, we were well enough satisfied with it for our quarters; and our landlady, who was the wife of some veteran serving abroad, knew well how to manage her house so as to make the most of it.

I shall here mention our usual meals (with which we were perfectly contented) during the time we were in quarters, as they differ so widely from what soldiers nowadays are accustomed to; premising, that we had our provisions, without contract, at our own purchasing. We breakfasted about nine in the morning, on bread and milk; dined about two in the afternoon, on potatoes and a couple of salt herrings, boiled in the pot with the potatoes: a bottle of small-beer (commonly called *swipes*) and a slice of bread served for supper, when we were disposed to take that meal, which soldiers seldom do. On the whole, I am certain our expenses for messing, dear as markets were, did not exceed three shillings and sixpence each, weekly; and to do our landlady justice, she was not anxious to encourage extravagance in preparing and cooking our meals, particularly such as required fuel and attention; and in these matters we were far from being troublesome or particular. Our obliging landlady would, when requested, bring us a pennyworth of soup, called *kale*, for our dinner, instead of herring; and if we had a little cause to remark on the want of cleanliness in the dish, or its contents, she jocosely replied, "It tak's a deal o' dirt to poison *sogers*."

After being quartered in this house a few weeks, the regiment was ordered into the Castle, which we occupied nearly two years. During this period (1804) the Leith wet-docks were forming, and gave employment to a great number of labourers as well as to soldiers. Such was the demand for willing hands, that not an idle man was to be found in the barracks, while these works were carrying on: all were actively employed, with the exception of those left for the purpose of duty. I was one of the latter class, and considered myself well paid by being allowed to mount guard for some of those at work, when it came to their turn of duty, as they seldom paid less than two shillings for each turn; and I was very saving of this money, on purpose to send to my mother a pound note occasionally; and by saving for her, I was also led on to save for myself. I had about fifteen pounds deposited in the hands of a friend when I entered the Militia, and before I left that corps for the Line, I had good bills for sixty.

I was also improving a little in personal appearance; short as the time had been since the regiment was embodied, I had sprung up a couple of inches, and was selected for the light company.

It would, perhaps, be improper to permit the system of working, just alluded to, to be carried on in the regular army, from which a pension becomes certain to the invalid; but where men are drawn from their homes merely for the purpose of being trained to arms, for the defence of their country upon any emergency, and no permanent benefit is expected to arise from the service otherwise, it is well to encourage in every individual, so drawn out, a spirit of industry. It is the means of enabling him to return improved in the avocation from which he may have been called, and with a resolution to benefit by increased information and experience.

I shall pass hastily over those scenes of every day occurrence, and place before my reader what may be considered of more interest.

From Edinburgh we marched to Haddington, where we remained upwards of a year. Our next removal was to Musselburgh, from which we sent detachments to do duty over the prisoners of war at Greenlaw. This was a light, and in some respects even an amusing duty. The prison was fenced round with a double row of stockades; a considerable space was appropriated as a promenade, where the prisoners had freedom to walk about, cook provisions, make their markets, and exercise themselves at their own pleasure, but under the superintendence of a turnkey and in the charge of several sentries.

The prisoners were locked up at sunset, and then the sentries, who were out of immediate view of the guardhouse, laid their firelocks against the sentry-boxes and amused themselves by playing at putting-stone, pitch-and-toss, and suchlike amusements, without fear of detection; for a cordial unity of feeling existed throughout the corps, so that as soon as the officer, sergeant, or corporal of the guard made his appearance, it was notified in an instant to the most remote corners, without his being aware of the communication, and our gambling amusements instantly ceased.

While our duty was thus easily and pleasantly performed, the prisoners of war under our charge were far from being severely treated, as some have stated; no work was required at their hands, yet few of them were idle. Some of them were occupied in culinary avocations, and as the guard had no regular mess, the men on duty became ready purchasers of their *labscuse**, salt-fish, potatoes, and coffee. Others were employed in preparing straw for plaiting; some were manufacturing the cast-away bones into dice, dominoes, paper-cutters, and a hundred articles of toy-work; while a considerable number were employed in vending these articles, and by this means realised considerable sums of money.

Thus time passed with the prisoners; they might have thought themselves well off, but in general they did not think so, for they were still prisoners, and longed to be again free.

I shall leave it to the political economist to determine, whether there was justice done to the country, or kindness shown to the prisoners, in keeping them thus shut up unemployed to public advantage. Those prisoners were well provided for in every respect, and treated with the greatest humanity; yet to the eye of a stranger they presented a miserable picture of distress, while some of them were actually hoarding up money by the most unjustifiable means, evading taxes to which our industrious artisans had to submit, and even forging our paper currency without being arraigned. Others were actually naked, with the exception of a dirty rag as an apron—some even destitute of this; and strangers who visited the prison commiserated the apparent distress

---

* *Labscuse* is a thick soup consisting of very little minced meat, a good seasoning of pepper, and plenty of potatoes. It may be said to be a dish between potato-soup and Irish stew.

of this miserable class, and charity was frequently bestowed on purpose to clothe their nakedness; but no sooner would this set of despicables obtain such relief, than they took to the cards, dice, or dominoes, and in a few hours were as poor and naked as ever.

From the wretched appearance of those gamesters, casual visitors and philanthropists concluded that the fault lay in the management; but a Howard could not have made these wretches more comfortable, without having recourse to strong coercive measures; for, strange as it may appear, when they were indulged with permission to remain in their hammocks, when the weather was cold, they drew the worsted out of the rugs that covered them, wound it up in balls, and sold it to the industrious knitters of *mitts,* and left themselves without a covering by night.

The inhabitants of Pennycuick and its neighbourhood, previous to the establishment of this depot of prisoners, were as comfortable and contented a class of people as in any district in Britain. The steep woody banks of the Esk were lined with prospering manufactories; neat houses and cleanly cottages rose on each side of the road leading to the village and overlooking the windings of the river. All these were tenanted by an industrious thriving community, principally paper-makers.

At these manufactories, the young as well as the old obtained employment according to their abilities, and liberal wages were given. Their hours of labour were generally from three or four in the morning until the same hour in the afternoon. This rendered it unnecessary to light candles during an)' part of the evening, either in summer or winter; and the leaving off work so early in the afternoon, afforded sufficient time for domestic labour or rural sports.

The cleanliness required in some of the departments of these manufactories, particularly that assigned to the women, was attended with the best effects, and displayed itself in the superior neatness and comfort of their dwellings; and no place could boast of women so decently, so genteelly, yet so unostentatiously dressed, as those on the lovely banks of the Esk.

At that time there were only one or two public-houses in Pennycuick, and none in Kirkhill, which contained nearly as many inhabitants; in short they were a thrifty, thriving, sober, well-disposed, kindly-hearted people.

When the soldiers (militiamen) were first quartered here, they met with a welcome reception, and were hospitably entertained: this was too frequently but poorly requited; and in the course of a few years, those kindly people began to consider the quartering of soldiers upon them more oppressive than they at first anticipated. Trade declined as prisoners increased; and instead of tradesmen's shops starting up into notice, public-houses were springing up, displaying the ill-drawn outlines of frothing jugs to the passengers and thirsty soldiers; while the latter, getting their provisions at a reasonable rate from the inhabitants, expended their pay in these houses, and too often led astray the younger branches of the families on whom they were billeted; and a laxity in the moral feelings and orderly habits of the rising generation visibly crept in.

One of the principal factories (Valleyfield) was afterwards converted into another depot for prisoners, and Esk-mills into a barrack for the military; this gave a decisive blow to trade, and several of the most active industrious young men emigrated to America, while others left their native home to carry the knowledge of their craft to other parts of the kingdom.

During the time that the regiment was quartered in Musselburgh, a general order was issued for the army to discontinue the tying of the hair, and to have it cropped. Never was an order received with more heartfelt satisfaction than this, or obeyed with more alacrity, notwithstanding the foolish predictions of some old superannuated gentlemen that it would cause a mutiny in the army. The tying was a daily penance, and a severe one, to which every man had to submit; and there is little doubt but this practice had been introduced by

35

some foreign fops, and enforced by antiquated prigs, as necessary to the cleanly appearance of the soldier. It had been very injurious in its effects on the general comforts of those who were obliged to submit to it, and the soldier looks back to the task with the painful remembrance of the punishment he suffered every morning, daubing the side of his head with dirty grease, soap, and flour, until every hair stood like the burr of a thistle, and the back was padded and pulled so that every hair had to keep its due place; if one less subordinate than the rest chanced to start up in spite of grease, soap-lather, and flour, the poor man had to sit down and submit his head to another dressing, and afterwards parade for inspection among the defaulters of the regiment.

A certain latitude and longitude was assigned for the breadth and length of the queue, to which a gauge was frequently applied, in the same manner as some modern sticklers for uniformity, at this day, use a measure to ascertain the dimensions of the soldiers' folded greatcoats at guard-mounting; but with this difference, the coat receives no bad impression from the stickler's gauge, whereas the greased and powdered hair retained the mark, and the poor fellow who had the misfortune to have the powder brushed aside by his awkward inspector, stood a chance of being turned off parade to have his hair dressed afresh, just as if the unlucky mark rendered him unfit for any military movement, or divested him of all the requisites of a soldier.

Indeed it was no uncommon circumstance for us, when on the guard-bench and asleep, to have the rats and mice scrambling about our heads, eating the filthy stuff with which our hair was bedaubed. We now look back to that time with a feeling of contempt at the absurdity of that detestable custom, and bless the memory of that prince who emancipated us from such an annoying and filthy practice.

It is an old saying and a true one, "Long wars make good soldiers." They not only make good soldiers, but they make good commanders, and enable them practically to know what is most conducive to the soldier's health, as well as to his efficiency for the service. The cropping of the hair was followed, some years afterwards, by an order for discontinuing the wear of white breeches on service. A gentleman, who had a servant to perform his work and assist in the arrangement of his dress, might have thought white small-clothes very suitable for a soldier; but they were neither pleasant, cleanly, nor comfortable to him; for the least stain appeared upon them, and the coarse quality of the cloth put washing with pure water and soap out of the question; they had therefore to be rubbed full of pipe-clay and whitening, so as almost to blind the poor man so employed with the dust. Here we had a fair exterior for a field-day; but if the weather was hot, the perspiration and whitening fretted and prickled our thighs; if it rained, the cloth becoming saturated, the pipe-clay dust was little better than quicklime; if the streets were dirty, the woeful marks flew from our heels to our breech, as if some wicked elf had followed with a paint-brush.

But setting aside these serious annoyances, they were generally made so tight and braced up so firm, that we almost stood like automata of wood, mechanically arranged for some exhibition on a large scale. To stoop was more than our small-clothes were worth; buttons flying, knees bursting, back parts rending; and then the long heavy groan when we stood up, just like an old corpulent gouty man after stooping to lift his fallen crutch.

Prom Musselburgh the regiment marched to Edinburgh, whence, after a twelvemonth's stay, it was ordered to Berwick, a fortified town on the north bank of the Tweed. The sea beats with great violence along this part of the coast, and notwithstanding that it presents a bold rocky front to the ocean, it is yielding to the never-ceasing action of the waves, which have undermined and broken down the adjoining banks in some places to a considerable extent.

Until Scotland and England acknowledged one sovereign, Berwick was one of the most important military posts in Great Britain, and more blood was perhaps shed in its neighbourhood than in the vicinity of any other town in either country. Happily for both countries, and no less so for Berwick, those deadly feuds have ceased since the two countries became united.

Berwick is a county of itself, independent of Scotland, yet gives name to the neighbouring shire, of which Greenlaw is the county town. It is connected with Tweedmouth, a large dependent suburb, by a bridge of fifteen arches. The town being considered in England, notwithstanding its situation on the north side of the river, is governed after the manner of other English towns. A mayor, recorder, town-clerk, and four aldermen form its magistracy; it is under the ecclesiastical authority of the Church of England, and in the diocese of Durham, to the prelate of which great honour is paid, on his occasional visitations to the place.

Marriages are performed at the Scotch toll-bar in the neighbourhood, in the same manner as at Gretna, and as frequently.

In no part of Britain have the young women a more stately carriage of body, than in this place and neighbourhood. This may be not a little owing to the manner in which they are accustomed to carry the water-pitcher, or *laglin,* on their heads, from the cistern or well; which custom invariably requires a steady step and an erect carriage, while that of carrying the pitchers or pails by their sides gives to the body an awkward and stooping gait, not easily thrown off.

There is something peculiar in the manner in which the natives *hurl* over the pronunciation of the letter *r;* this is called "the Berwick *burr,*" and prevails from Ayton to Alnwick; and some consider it as giving a pleasant though somewhat childish effect to the dialect.

From Berwick the regiment furnished a detachment to Holy Island Castle, about nine miles distant. Here are the extensive ruins of an ancient monastery, part of which serves for a parish-church. On the beach, below the castle; are found small pebbles of the shape of beads, half-perforated, and about the size of peas; the inhabitants call them St. Cuthbert's beads. Some seriously affirm that the monks of this monastery, under the patronage of St. Cuthbert, carried on a most extensive traffic in the sale of consecrated beads, and not only drew immense wealth to the shrine of the saint, but were enabled to remit a considerable revenue to the papal treasury. It happened, however, about two centuries before the reformation, that a small bark loaded with the half-finished material was wrecked on approaching the roadstead without a pilot, and the scattered half-perforated drops, now found along the beach, are alleged to be part of the sacred freight. Such at least is the traditional story in the island.

Near the entrance of the church is a large stone, over which it is customary for a bride to leap when she is going to be married, or after the ceremony is performed. If she leap freely and without stumbling, it is considered an omen of future comfort in the married life; if otherwise, the contrary.

From Berwick we removed to Dalkeith, from which a strong detachment was sent to do duty over the prisoners of war at Greenlaw and Valleyfield. My friend Huntly had been promoted some time previously to be a corporal, and perhaps with this small step of promotion his ambition soared; and as little prospect of further advancement appeared to gratify his views, he determined to volunteer his service to the Line. His remark was:

"I serve at present secure of life and limb, but with no prospect of future benefit in old age, which I may attain; it is better to hazard both abroad in the regular service, than have poverty and hard labour accompanying me to a peaceful grave at home."

I concurred in his opinion, and he forthwith waited on the commanding officer and signified his intention to volunteer into any regiment which that officer might be pleased to recommend. The offer was accepted in the most favourable manner, consequently my friend placed his name on the list for the 42nd (the regiment recommended), and I was not the last to follow the example; several others added their names to the roll, and after a few weeks, we were despatched to join the depot of the regiment at Inverness.

CHAPTER 4

Off to War

On our arrival at Inverness, we were offered a furlough for two months, an indulgence usually granted to volunteers from the Militia.

I have mentioned that Huntly was a corporal when he volunteered; he had not been aware, until this offer of a furlough was made, that he could not be borne on the strength of the regiment otherwise than as a private. He did not consider this, in common speaking, "fair play." Had he been detained as a supernumerary, without the pay, he would have been satisfied, as this would have given him some hopes of succeeding to a vacancy, but that was denied; he therefore declined taking a furlough, trusting that he would be sent out with the first *draught,* to join the battalion serving in Spain. He stated to the officer commanding the depot his reason for declining the proffered indulgence, at the same time expressing his disappointment at being reduced. The officer heard him with patience, perhaps with some feeling of sympathy, but held out no prospect of his being reappointed.

A soldier who has been once considered deserving of promotion, and has attained it, ought to be very tenacious in retaining it; if he is deprived of it by means of his own misconduct, he has himself to blame; but he who is unexpectedly reduced without a fault, and left without a prospect of being reappointed, may be justified in making an appeal to his commanding officer.

Huntly thought he had shewn sufficient cause why he should not be reduced from the little rank he had acquired, but he was mistaken; however, as he had attained that rank without solicitation, he was determined not to lose it without a struggle. He was one of those who was thought to regard passive obedience as a virtue in a soldier; but when it came to himself for trial, he spurned it as a detestable vice, fit only for slaves. He appealed to that officer at whose instance he had made choice of this regiment; the appeal was condescendingly received, and as favourably answered. In short, there being a vacant sergeantcy at the time, my friend was appointed to it, by the order of the most noble the Marquis of Huntly, colonel of the regiment. Huntly was thus far successful through the advocacy and recommendation of that officer, and I feel confident he will never disgrace that recommendation. I may be permitted to add, that I was promoted at the same time.

It is certainly not a little vexatious to an old soldier to see a young one stepping in before him for promotion, and thus depriving him of the expected reward of hard service. Yet had it been our worse fortune to have been kept back in rank, we would not have considered the officer then in command as having acted unjustly towards us; we had reason, however, to congratulate ourselves on our success.

I accepted of two months' furlough, and after passing the time as is usual on occasions of this kind, returned to Inverness, from which, in a few days, I was ordered to Edinburgh along with a party on the recruiting service.

Notwithstanding my having been so lately on furlough, I requested permission to proceed to Edinburgh by Huntly and Aberdeen. This is nearly seventy miles farther than by the Highland road (the route laid down for the party); and some doubt was consequently entertained by the officer commanding, of my being able to march by that circuitous route so as to arrive at Edinburgh as soon as the others; however, on my promising to be there on the day stated, if not sooner,

I received permission, and set out that afternoon, accompanied by four young men ordered to join recruiting parties stationed on that line of road.

Our knapsacks contained our complete *kits** as well as our new greatcoats, and were far from being light; but our hearts were not heavy nor our limbs feeble; we travelled all night and reached Keith a little past noon next day, a distance of fifty-six miles. My companions having little farther to go, in order to reach their respective parties, remained in Keith next day, while I set out alone to Huntly, whence, after calling on a few friends, and bidding them farewell, I proceeded to Inverury. This was a journey of more than thirty miles that day. Next morning I reached Aberdeen, where my mother had been some years residing; here I rested five days, and on the sixth proceeded on my journey. I reached Montrose about sunset, having thus travelled thirty-seven miles. The next day I travelled to Kirkcaldy, a distance of forty miles. I cannot say that I had any necessity for thus pressing forward, but as I now considered myself a soldier in reality, and having promised to be in Edinburgh as soon as the party that was marching by the shorter route, I was determined to inure myself to fatigue and privation, so that I might have less cause to consider these distressing if they should come upon me unexpectedly.

I may also observe, that in performing this journey I wore a sort of hose termed *moggans;* these are hose from which the feet have been cut, the spats cover this deficiency, and the legs appear as if the under parts were complete. This was an excellent method for hardening the feet, so as to accustom them to bad shoes and bad roads. I cannot say, however, that I was singular in adopting this plan of wearing feetless hose; for I afterwards observed, on joining the regiment, that very few of the men wore any other kind, although they had complete ones in their possession.

---

* *Kit* is a term used for the whole that a soldier is obliged to carry hi his knapsack, shirts, stockings, shoes, brushes, &c. &c.

I arrived at Edinburgh on the 6th September, but the party from which I had separated at Inverness did not arrive until the third day after.

I had formed an early acquaintance, while in the Militia, with a young girl, whom I greatly esteemed. In her I saw all that was good and agreeable. Years had elapsed since we had seen each other, and fortunately I chanced to meet her on my arrival; fortunately, I may say, for so it has proved; we were mutually surprised at seeing each other, and truly happy. In a few months she became my wife, and has shared with me in all my fortunes, over field and flood, in camp and in quarters, in war and in peace, without any unpleasant reflection at her own share of suffering.

After passing about eight months on the recruiting service, I was ordered to Inverness, where, after remaining a few days, I embarked along with the draught, on purpose to join the first battalion, serving in Spain. We had a pleasant coasting voyage to Gravesend, where we disembarked and marched to Portsmouth; here transports were in readiness to take a number of troops out to reinforce the army.

We embarked on the 17th August, 1813, along with a detachment of cavalry and a detachment of the 79th regiment, and stood out to sea. Calms and gentle breezes favoured us until we reached the Spanish coast and cast anchor at the mouth of the Ybaichalval, where the cavalry disembarked, and our captain commanding on board went on shore, on purpose to proceed to Bilboa, situated a few miles up that river, whence he was to proceed to join us at Passages, where we were to land. On the removal of the cavalry, our accommodation between decks was considerably enlarged, as the space vacated was taken possession of immediately. This being all settled, the call was given for "Rum;"* a call to which every

---

* Every soldier on board is allowed one-third of a pint of rum daily. Some commanding officers cause it to be reduced to two or three-water grog, before serving out. I cannot say how far this is necessary for the men's health; but I know it is not liked by the men, and I never saw those grog recommenders take it themselves.

ear was open, and a hundred voices repeated it from stem to stern, and a busy bustling scene ensued and continued for some minutes afterwards.

The acting quartermaster-sergeant of the 42nd on board, had been the only individual whose conduct during the voyage tended to give displeasure; but this displeasure had not been openly manifested. He was a mean, tippling, talkative little fellow, and had been daily on the watch, during the voyage, to have the first issue of spirits for the men on his draught. He was the more importunate in demanding it as a right of seniority, as he thought he should be supported by the captain commanding, who belonged to the same corps. But when the captain left the transport, the men of the 79th did not feel inclined to yield any longer to this assumed demand; and when our busy sergeant, who had been engaged below assigning convenient berths to his dram-giving favourites, presented himself on deck, the acting quartermaster-sergeant of the 79th was being served. This the officious little fellow would by no means allow, and an altercation took place, which induced the officer who succeeded to the command to interpose, and our insubordinate hero treating that officer's authority with contempt, was placed under arrest, and on joining the regiment, was tried by a court-martial and reduced to the ranks.

It is sometimes the case that a soldier of the lowest estimation, by his ill-timed boasting, will excite a spirit of bad feeling between two regiments; but when disrespect or contempt is openly manifested by a non-commissioned officer, especially if he be a somewhat leading personage among his equals, towards the officers of another corps, it seldom fails to lead to an open rupture, if not timely suppressed, and every man of the corps to which the strife-stirring individual belongs, ought to spurn him from his presence as a general nuisance. Indeed our men had become ashamed of this tippling sergeant's behaviour, and the whisper had been for some days, that our friends' of the 79th displayed a very praiseworthy forbearance, in not resenting the conduct of this officious character; and instead of supporting him, we were ready to censure his unjustifiable proceedings.

Let us be ever so much addicted to drinking or drunkenness ourselves, we never fail to consider it as a vice, condemn it in our inferiors, despise it in our equals, and most cordially join in speaking disrespectfully of a superior addicted to it.

We landed at Passages on the 7th September, and proceeded without delay to Ranturea; here an old convent was assigned for our quarters, and we occupied it two nights. The courts and lower part of the building were taken up by batmen, muleteers, and bullock-drivers, with their horses, mules, asses, and oxen. The dilapidated apartments above were assigned for the quarters of the soldiers, who found it necessary to unhinge the doors and window-shutters, on purpose to cover the joists, from which the flooring had been torn up for fuel. The slabs were raised from the lobbies and courts below, and laid in the centre of the upper rooms, for the purpose of fire-places. Thus, by hasty devastations, this once revered abode of monks, friars, and priests was exposed to every kind of pollution, blackened with the smoke of a hundred fires, fed by its own altars and furniture, and the walls left a naked monument of the ravages of war.

If the confusion of Babel was bad, this was worse. Below, the tinkling of mule-bells never ceased, the neighing of the horse was answered by the braying of the mules and asses; the bellowing of the half-starved oxen mingled with these, and echoed through every room and vault of the building; while the loud and frequent exclamations of "*Carachue!*" by the muleteers, gave no rest but to such as were totally overpowered with sleep. Indeed a number of the men were far from being disposed to rest; some having indulged themselves too freely in the juice of the grape, or the more pernicious libations of *aquadent,** heretofore unknown to them, were brawling inces-

---

* *Aquadent* is an ardent spirit distilled from the refuse of the grape, raisins, and aniseed.

santly; others were disposed for singing and merriment; while exclamations of "D—n you, keep silence!" burst from twenty mouths at once.

Amidst this scene of uproar, some poor luckless *wight*, with disordered stomach and bowels, was scrambling on all-fours, groping his passage to the door, getting a kick from one and an oath from another, till unable in the darkness to find egress, he discharged his unwelcome burden upon some one asleep and dreaming perhaps of the waves dashing against the prow of the vessel from which he so lately debarked, and in which he thinks himself still a passenger, till one surge sweeps the deck, breaks over his head, and starts him from his dream, when, to his inexpressible surprise, he finds himself besmeared by the evacuations of a bewildered comrade.

Thus passed the hours usually devoted to sleep, while the distant booming of the battering-train laying siege to St. Sebastian, apprized us of our proximity to the scene of hostilities, in which we ourselves might be soon called upon to engage.

Welcome morning came at last. Ah! how we poor soldiers do anticipate time! We lie down after the fatigues of the day, happy that they are over, yet our minds full of the concerns of to-morrow; the morning comes, and we wish for the night, as if time did not fly swift enough to bring us to the close of our duty, our servitude, and life.

We here met with a corporal, who had been sent from his regiment on purpose to purchase shoes at Passages for the men of his company. A fleet having arrived from England, this was just the time to obtain a supply, and the men were in great want of that article: had he proceeded without delay in order to obtain the first advantage, he might have succeeded with some credit to himself and satisfaction to the shoeless men; but he was one of those who sacrifice duty to their selfish pleasures, and instead of proceeding as he ought to have done, he hung about our party until he was incapable, and thus lost an opportunity of making a good purchase. In this manner a number of drunken *scamps* left their duty unperformed, and returned with some plausible apology for the want of success.

A soldier ought to form very few acquaintances, for by the multiplicity of his connexions his duty is liable to be compromised; it becomes an intolerable burden, is neglected, perhaps abandoned altogether; and he becomes a curse to his corps, and an enemy to the best interests of his country.

After resting two nights at Ranturea, we proceeded to Lazzaca, at that time the head-quarters of Lord Wellington.

Our captain, who had left us at the mouth of the Ybaichalval, joined us at Passages, and took the command. This officer had served a campaign in Portugal along with the second battalion of the regiment, and considered himself more knowing in military affairs than the young officers who were under his command; but whatever knowledge he might have acquired in military tactics, he betrayed a great want of geographical information, at least so far as regarded the topography of that part of the country in which we were now about to be stationed; for instead of leading us on the direct road to Lazzaca, he marched us along the straight road to Bayonne, until our advanced picquets convinced him of his error. In order to remedy this mistake, he procured a guide, and made a retrograde movement that brought us to a road similar to the dried up channel of a mountain torrent. This rugged path, by which we now proceeded, was narrow, winding, and in some places almost impervious; one false step from our path, in those places, would have been instant death, so steep was the declivity to our right, that human foot had never marked its side, or reached in safety the gulf-like bottom.

At times the eye was gratified with the most romantic views; but soldiers, almost breathless and panting beneath the burden of arms, ammunition, accoutrements, and heavy knapsacks, felt but little pleasure in feasting their eyes on such scenes of solitary grandeur.

In several places we found the traces of recent encampments, distinguishable by the few huts that still remained on the spot, and the blasted appearance of the woods in the vicinity, the trees presenting their naked, leafless, blackened branches, as if drooping under the spell of some necromancer. The huge trunks were excavated and rent by the camp-fires that had been lighted under their ample shades. The abrupt craggy knolls, which frequently half-encircled those table fields, raised their summits, like watch-towers, on high, while their rents and rifts were clustered with dwarf trees, ferns, and shrubs, the yellow leaves of which hid the nakedness of the rocks in which they were rooted.

Evening was approaching as we entered Lazzaca, and we found in it a scene of activity beyond anything we had as yet observed; the streets were lined with innumerable fires, at which the soldiers and followers of the army had been cooking, and some were still occupied in their culinary avocations; troops of mules were passing and re-passing, others loading or unloading, while not a few were enjoying their provender, and their guides reposing under the arcade of some adjoining building.

Our day's march over, we had now to look out for our next day's provisions. The commissary stores being nearly a league further, a small party of us had to proceed thither to draw the rations; on our arrival, we found the bullocks alive, and the butchers about to retire to rest, and not over willing to recommence work. I think the men so employed belonged to the Guards, and it is but justice to say, that they did their work cleverly, exclaiming as they stripped to perform, "We shall not let the poor Highlanders wait long for our service." And they were as good as their word; we were grumbling much at the distance we had been obliged to come, but the sympathizing expression of "poor Highlanders" warmed our hearts towards the Guardsmen, so that our disregarded grumbles ceased at once.

When the spirits, however, were measuring out, a considerable hole was observed in the measure, which occasioned a fresh grumble, I may say an uproar, for it was nearly all issued before the fraud was detected. The place where the issue was made was lit with one dim glimmering light, and the liquor, previous to being measured out, was drawn off into a large tub, in which the measure was immersed, filled to the lip, apparently good measure, but the hole let off more than two men's share in every gallon. We were always particularly tenacious of good measure when we were receiving, though we felt no scruple in dipping our own thumbs pretty deep into the measure with which we made the distribution, justifying ourselves no doubt, in so doing, as it were on purpose to prevent drunkenness and secure ourselves from loss; a very justifiable consideration on our own part, if we could get others also to think so, and allow us to be the distributors. Perhaps there are few frauds committed, but what the committer reasons with himself in this manner, till he believes he is acting laudably, notwithstanding that it displays a slight want of honesty.

After passing a night in a broken down convent, we left Lazzaca. I say *passing*, for of rest we had none, in consequence of a fire having been lit, by some careless fellow, on the floor of one of the rooms which was boarded, and caught the fire, and set us in a bustle to put down the flames before the alarm spread; happily we succeeded, and the whole party marched off in the morning without detection.

We now proceeded on a good road to St. Stephano, a small town situated in a delightful valley, through which the Bidasoa winds its course, overhung with woods, or lined with pleasant fields, fruitful orchards and gardens, which happily had escaped the ravages of the contending armies, and the visits of marauders from the craving camps.

On the following day we marched to Allesander; here a number of hospitals were established for the sick and wounded of the army, and detachments of British soldiers were moving from the interior of Spain, where they had been detained by wounds, sickness, or duty, but now about to join their respective corps.

We were now approaching the scene of hostilities, and perceived different parties of foragers ranging the country, and cutting down the abandoned harvest. Some of those parties belonged to the camp, others to the commissariat. The batmen of the respective brigades composed the camp foragers; and these, in looking out for provender for their animals, furnished themselves by stealth with any useful portable article they could conveniently slip into their haversacks, so as to be carried off with impunity from the houses which they sometimes visited. The foragers belonging to the commissariat consisted principally of Portuguese, escorted by some soldiers. These roved over the country, purchasing livestock, as well as other necessary-stores for the provisioning of the army; but it may be observed, that in bargaining, more attention was paid to individual interest than to public advantage or quick dispatch. Cattle were bought from the farmers and resold with impunity; for the purchaser paid in promissory checks on the commissary, and the value of those checks depended merely on the success of our arms, consequently could not be considered otherwise than doubtful. The farmer, therefore, upon receiving back his cattle, by a secret compromise, gave back the checks, and a considerable sum to boot; the party then proceeded to another farm, to drive fresh bargains, harass the country, and delay the supplies. It was not a little owing to this sort of dealing, that our provisions were of so inferior a quality to what might have been procured.

The road continues good from Allesander until we reach Mayo, a small village which gives name to one of the mountain passes. From this village we ascended the heights on which the sixth division of the army was encamped, and there terminated our route as a draught from the second battalion.

CHAPTER 5

My First Sight of Battle

After being named off to our respective companies in the regiment, we were conducted to our tents. Here we were surrounded by a number of inquisitive soldiers, some congratulating us on our arrival, others enquiring for old acquaintances left behind, and not a few desirous to know what the public opinion at home was concerning the operations of the army of which we now formed a part.

I perceived my fellow-travellers beginning to open their budgets of letters, in order to put them in circulation; as for myself I had none to deliver, and I began to think that I had been rather careless, on leaving the second battalion, in not soliciting, from a well-wisher or friend, some recommendatory letter, so as to secure me the good opinion of a superior, or at least an equal, to whom I might appeal for support or apply for advice in the event of wanting either. It was too late, however, to remedy any neglect, and I cannot say, now when writing this, that I have much occasion to regret that omission; for, though my path has not been strewed with roses, it has not been so thorny as to stop my advance.

Before I proceed further in my narrative, I shall make a few preliminary remarks, and trust that, in so doing, I need offer no apology for some animadversions that may follow regarding the conduct of individuals, as it is by pointing out errors that we know how to avoid them, and by concealing them from view, if we do not injure, we certainly do not benefit those who are to tread in the same path. The necessary restrictions placed upon a soldier certainly prevent him from coming forward to accuse one placed over him of petty acts of oppression, such as a man in civil life would not suffer without resenting. It is not to be thought, however, that the former feels less the indignity or the sting of degradation, although he does not retaliate, and dare not avenge. It is therefore a mean cowardly action for one placed in power to pride himself in insulting or brow-beating a man who dares not retaliate without committing a crime, and incurring certain punishment. That such overbearing conduct was common in some regiments, cannot be denied, indeed it was too general; but I confine my remarks to that which has come under my own observation in the regiment to which I now belong, trusting that should they ever meet the eye of one of those who pride themselves in looking on an inferior with contempt, he will correct himself and act in a more manly manner in future.

I shall not be prolix in my encomiums upon the regiment's superiority in discipline to that of others; indeed I cannot; to say the truth, it was rather lax in this respect. Colonel Stirling commanded the regiment at the time I joined it; but in a few days thereafter, he resigned the command, went to England, and was appointed major-general. On his leaving the regiment, the command devolved on Lieutenant-Colonel Macara, a brave man, who feared no personal danger, but was not well acquainted with field manoeuvres or military tactics. This might have been owing, in a great measure, to his predecessor seldom having been absent from the regiment; so that not having the command sooner, he had not the opportunity of perfecting himself, by that practice which is absolutely necessary for one about to lead a regiment into the field.

It is a well known fact, that the most active officer in a regiment, if he has never been in front of the parade to take command, makes but a very awkward display of his abilities, on his first attempt to conduct the movements of a battalion: such appeared to be the case with Colonel Macara when he assumed the command, and this was at a time, and in a place, presenting many obstacles to his improving himself by practice.

First, the ruggedness of the mountains prevented precision of movements; secondly, the weather had become so unfavourable that every fair day was dedicated to some other necessary purpose about the camp, and instead of acquiring practical knowledge himself, even his regiment was losing part of that which it had perhaps previously possessed; thirdly, draughts of undisciplined recruits were occasionally joining and mixing in the ranks, and being unaccustomed to field movements, occasioned a sort of awkwardness in the performance of them.

Even after our return from the continent, when the regiment was quartered in Ireland, many obstacles started up unfavourable to field practice, namely, old soldiers and limited service men being discharged, the second battalion joining, the principal part of which were recruits, and men who had been years in French prisons; the detached state of the regiment, after all these had been squad drilled, left but few soldiers at head-quarters to enable the commanding officer to practise with. In this manner we continued until the battle of Waterloo, when his fall at Quatre-Bras threw a halo round his expiring command, which places him on the list of our bravest countrymen.

Lieutenant Innes performed the duty of adjutant; he was an excellent officer, particularly correct in the management of regimental business and arrangement of duties. I cannot be mistaken in saying that he was a good man, for I never heard a bad one speak well of him, for he was an enemy of bad men; but the most worthless could not but allow afterwards, when he fell on the battlefield, that he left not a braver behind.

Clark was our sergeant-major—a good, kindly-hearted, brave soldier. Some may think me too prolix in my details, by giving a place to the sergeant-major, passing over names of higher rank and greater consequence; but to a soldier this needs no apology, for he knows that the commanding officer, the adjutant, and the sergeant-major are the mainsprings which set all the regimental machinery in motion. Indeed, it is notorious the influence that some sergeant-majors have in their respective corps. If the commanding officer be of an easy complying turn, or of a repulsive, haughty, *don't-trouble-me* disposition, and the adjutant, which is often the case, not over well informed, the sergeant-major is consulted on all occasions; if a man be confined or reported for some misconduct or occasional neglect, the sergeant-major's opinion will be asked as to character, which he may establish or injure at pleasure, for who will be called upon to contradict him, especially if a few trifling incidents be adduced by him in support of what he has stated.

In short, he was much more to say between the non-commissioned officers and commanding officer regarding the poor soldier's conduct than all the captains and subalterns of the regiment. A drill-sergeant has not a little in his power, in forming good or bad principles in the young recruit; and I am sorry to say that, for the most part, the regiment was much at a loss in this respect, so far as regarded the formation of a sober character. As I may have occasion to revert to this subject in the course of the following pages, I shall return to the camp and the concerns connected with the regiment and the duties I had to perform.

On joining the regiment, I considered my duties with the draught at a close; but in this I was disappointed, for the regiment having previously received rations for the following day, it became necessary to issue the same allowance to the draught, and this duty fell upon me to perform. I was assisted in drawing the quantity, and in the distribution, by one of the corporals. We had also a number of generous obliging old soldiers, all strangers to us, but extremely willing to serve in distributing the provisions, not only on our own account, but on that of those who had lately arrived; yet with all this assistance, we were deficient of bread and meat for three besides myself; the captain was one of the three, and the most dis-contented at the deficiency. I was not a little puzzled how to make up the loss, as there was no such thing as meat to be got for money. Luckily the quartermaster-sergeant was at hand, and called me aside and obligingly made up the loss; thus all our affairs were settled satisfactorily.

I cannot pass over this disinterested act of kindness, done to me by this generous man, without a painful feeling at his early exit from this war-breathing, peace-seeking world. He now rests in the grave of his fathers, alike unconscious of the praise of a friend and the censure of a foe; and in paying this small acknowledgment to his memory, I have no other purpose to serve than to bring his forgotten merits to the recollection of those who have seen him, but knew not the goodness of his heart.

Fraser was but an enlisted boy in the regiment, when he was taken notice of by Colonel Stirling for his regular, quiet, sober, yet active manner of conducting himself; he was sent to school, and afterwards appointed schoolmaster-sergeant, the first, I believe, in the regiment; but when the battalion was ordered abroad, he declined remaining at home, went out with it, did the duty of quartermaster-sergeant, and I may add, that of quartermaster also, for both these functionaries, soon after their arrival in the Peninsula, obtained leave to return to Britain, and a subaltern officer was nominally ap-pointed for the latter duty, while to all intents and purposes Fraser performed both, so far as not to intrude himself where the superior was required or demanded. In his behaviour, he was sedate, without sullenness; cheerful, convivial, and full of jocularity, without intemperance or injuring the object of his mirth. He was master of a Masonic lodge held in the regi-ment, and happening to observe the arms of that body cut on the mess-tin I had on my knapsack, he took me for a brother, and acted as one towards me, until death robbed the regi-ment of one of the best of its men, and myself of a kindly and warm-hearted friend.

After having seen the provisions distributed, I set about looking out for some accommodation for my wife, for we had not as yet been accustomed to lie on the open field, as in bivouac, nor even seen the like, and the tent was far from comfortable for a poor, wearied, young woman; I shall not mention delicacy, for that would be out of place; we must submit to circumstances. The names of seventeen men were on the roll of the tent besides myself, so it may be easily guessed how crowded it must have been, had the whole been off duty, but this was seldom the case. However, as no other shelter was to be had, we took a berth under it.

Eleven soldiers lay in it that night along with us, all stretched with their feet to the centre and their heads to the curtain of the tent, every man's knapsack below his head, and his clothes and accoutrements on his body; the one half of the blankets under, and the other spread over the whole, so that we all lay in one bed. Often did my poor wife look up to the thin canvas that screened her face from the night-dew, and wish for the approaching morn. It was announced at last, before daybreak, by an exclamation of "Rouse!" which passed from tent to tent along the lines, when every man started up, folded his blanket, and strapped it on the back of his knapsack, ready for a march, and soon afterwards the sound of bugle and drum echoed from hill to hill; meanwhile the army stood to arms, each regiment at its alarm post, until about sunrise.

The view from the summits of these mountains, at that early hour, when the sun began to gild their tops, and to throw his cheering rays on the white canvas which speckled their sides, was grand beyond description. The valleys below were hidden under an ocean of white wreathing mist, over which the hills, like a thousand islands, raised their rocky summits amidst the pure serenity of a cloudless atmosphere; the white tents of a British army spotted their sides, while ten thousand bayonets littered around. The drums, fifes, bugles, and wild warlike strains of the Highland bagpipe, drowned the notes of a hundred useless instruments that offered their softer sounds to the soldiers' ears. Flocks of vultures hovered around to feed on the bodies of men who had fallen in sequestered spots by the hostile bullet, and were left to wolves and birds of prey, along with the carcases of the exhausted animals that had failed in bearing their oppressive burdens to the expectant camp.

As the sun rose over the mountains, the misty vapours rolled away, and all the vales, woods, streams, and distant cottages appeared to view. What a lovely prospect this must have been to the once happy native of the soil! Those hills, once covered with flocks of sheep; those valleys, where the herds of cattle were richly fed, and the husbandman reared the vine, the olive, the fig, the lime the orange, and all the fruits peculiar to a genial soil and a salubrious climate; those woods which once rung with the voice of gladness, and echoed to the music of a happy, contented, peaceful peasantry; and those cottages, once their cherished abode—all these I now behold spread out beneath me, and I think I see an aged man, whose respectable appearance bespeaks him to have witnessed better days, mourning over the scene, bewailing the fate of his country, and dropping a tear over his own misery. Those hills are now covered with warlike encampments, and in place of herds of cattle, columns of soldiers move along the valleys. The vines and the fruit-trees are cut down for fuel; the wood falls on every side beneath the soldiers' hatchets, and reverberates the voice of revelry. The cottages, which once appeared as white as the snow that covers the top of Ben-Nevis, are stained with the smoke of surrounding fires, while the owner stands afar off, in his secret retreat, beholding the desolation that surrounds his once happy dwelling; perhaps some straggler of his flock strays to its wonted haunts, and he sees it fall a victim beneath the knife of a foreign soldier. He beholds all this, and with a bursting heart and tearful eye he turns to fly from the scene of ruin. Alas! whither shall he fly? he has no home; his fields are laid waste; his flocks and herds have already become the prey of strangers, while his family and friends are scattered abroad or fallen by the random bullet; he stands a lonely unprotected being on the surface of his native soil, his heart bursting with grief, and no kind friend, his equal in misfortune, to condole with him in his sorrows, nor any generous protector to alleviate his distress.

The troops being dismissed to their tents, after their morning muster, every man was busily employed in some duty or other.

I now set about erecting a hut for myself and wife, resolving, if possible, not to mix blankets with so many bedfellows again. This I was the more anxious to do, because at that time the whole of the men were affected with an eruption on their skin similar to the itch, and their clothing was in a very filthy state*, owing to its being seldom shifted, and always kept on during the night.

With the assistance of a few willing hands, I finished the hut in the course of the day, so that it served for a temporary shelter, and prevented myself and wife from depriving the men of their very limited accommodation in the tent. When I stretched myself down at night, in my new habitation, my head rested against the one end while my feet touched the other, at which was the entrance; my wife's apron being hung up as a substitute for a door, a couple of pins on each side served for lock and hinges; and feeble as that barrier was, none of the men entered when that was suspended, and we might have left it to its own keeping from morning till night without an article being abstracted: thieving, indeed, was unknown in the regiment; but, in fact, there was little of worth to steal amongst us.

Our men, in general, were possessed of another praiseworthy disposition, they were obliging without being troublesome or intrusive; and any errors or crimes amongst them

---

* There seems to be something peculiarly favourable in the Spanish soil towards the production of one of the insect plagues of Egypt. For I have seen linen, perfectly clean, laid down on the bank of a remote stream to bleach, and, when lifted, having become the residence of some very unwelcome visitors.

invariably originated from drunkenness, a vice of so long standing in all armies, thatit has been passed over, by the best commanders, with slight arbitrary punishments, when not attended with aggravating circumstances.

The first duty I performed, after joining the regiment, was mounting the quarter guard; and one of the men belonging to it absented himself and returned drunk, noisy, and very troublesome, with his mighty boastings of what he had seen and suffered; reminding me of what Homer says of the Greeks:

Each fearless hero dares a hundred foes,
While the feast lasts, and while the goblet flows.

It may be justifiable in a poor fellow to boast of his own merit, when he finds it entirely neglected by others, or hidden from the cheering ray of regimental patronage, that falls so fortunately upon some individuals, whose superficial show reflects more brilliantly the beam that animates their hopes and cherishes their growing ambition. Yet, there is a limit to which a soldier's boasting should be confined, for when it exceeds that, it becomes offensive. I had only been a few days in the regiment, and had therefore no just cause to take any slighting aspersions thrown at me as really personal; but as the man was unfit for duty, it became mine to confine him; and having done this, I was almost overwhelmed with a torrent of abuse; for there was a mistaken idea entertained, that a soldier in confinement might commit an outrage on the person or character of another, and only be answerable for that for which he was committed.

I was, much to my satisfaction, relieved from my unpleasant situation by the visiting officer for the day (Lieutenant D. Farquharson), who happened to be going his rounds, and ordered the prisoner to keep silence. This command changed the course of the torrent from me towards that gentleman, on whom it burst with redoubled violence.

I had not in the course of my ten years' previous service witnessed a soldier drunk on guard, but it came under my observation on the first I mounted in the regiment; yet none of the men seemed the least surprised at the crime, or astonished at the abusive language the prisoner made use of; they even seemed to think such ebullitions of passion as the hereditary privilege of an old soldier, and of no uncommon occurrence among them.

The presence of a formidable enemy, in front of our lines, tended to mitigate punishments, that under other circumstances might have been awarded, and allowed offenders to get off with very slight correctives, in order to prevent our ranks being thinned by avoidable casualties. The prisoner was released next day, and sentenced to undergo a few days' drill.

From what I had thus heard and seen, I considered that I had to be very cautious of incurring the displeasure of an old soldier—a false idea, which made me act too often in a manner that on a retrospective view I consider injudicious. I had good officers, however, and if I erred in judgment, it was not intentionally, neither was it laid to my charge as such, but passed over in silence, and I was left to my own self-contrition afterwards. Indeed, I am far from justifying tyranny in any class of society whatsoever; but I cannot help thinking that a little despotism must be blended with the disposition of the most liberal minded man who has to command others, whether he be a general or a lance-corporal; for the more concessions that are made to some, the more dissatisfaction will be the result, and in the end will lead to the degradation of him who meanly weakens his authority by his want of firmness in maintaining it.

On the 6th of October we advanced towards the heights of Urdach, and descended a few paces on the brow of that part of the mountain which overlooks the valley of that name and the distant course of the Neville. A thick cloud hovered beneath us, and hid the country from our view. The loud report of guns, in the valley, shook the hills and echoed throughout the dark woody ravines below, whilst the quick rounds of musketry prepared us to expect an order to descend to the scene of action. The division stood in columns of brigade, or in lines along the mountain paths, as the position could be taken up.

We remained upwards of two hours enveloped in the misty clouds, every man full of anxiety to view the contest below. At last our wishes were gratified; the curtain arose, and the interesting scene burst all at once on our view. A far discerning eye might see the skirmishers of both armies approaching close to each other, each man with well-directed aim looking along the deadly tube that sent the intended messenger of death to the opposing adversary. Vineyards, orchards, straggling bushy fences, and streamlets with steep banks intersected the country, and afforded occasional cover to both sides, as well as a rest to the marksman's musket in taking a deliberate aim. The ascent of the cloud, which had hovered beneath us and over the combatants, afforded them a view of our columns and lines ready to descend, a prospect no less discouraging to the enemy than animating to our friends; the former retired towards the Neville, while our troops pursued, till night closed the contest, and gave a respite from toil to both victor and vanquished.

CHAPTER 6

Into Battle

The distant action over, we returned to the heights above Mayo and occupied our old camp-ground for three successive nights. On the 9th of October we again advanced. Major Cowell, at the head of the light-infantry companies of the brigade, drove back the enemy's picquets and established our advances on the defiles of the mountains looking down towards France.

Without pushing the victory farther, the division encamped on the heights above Urdach. Here I erected a hut, larger than my former one, and more substantial. Having occupied that which I had left nearly four weeks, I considered, that if I were to occupy this the half of that time, I should be satisfied in bestowing more labour on it, and making my accommodation more complete; but rain continued to fall for two days in succession, and placed us in a very unpleasant situation. I had cut a trench round the outside of my hut, so as to carry off the torrents which rushed against it from the declivities above, and my poor wife was no less busily employed in securing the few articles within. "When the weather cleared, I set about re-thatching my new habitation, but the first night after I had finished my work, a violent gale struck every tent in the camp, and swept ray little hut completely off. I had thrown my blanket over it and fixed it down with cords and pegs, on purpose to secure the thatch; having thus secured the roof, or I may rather say my hut, for it was all roof and ends, we stretched ourselves down, and the roaring of the wind in a few minutes lulled us to sleep, for we felt confident of having made all secure. Our repose, however, was short; we were awakened by the feeble branches which composed the rafters falling on our heads, and on looking up, no roof sheltered us from the blast. The stars shone brightly between the flying clouds, and the busy hum of a thousand voices rose on the wind as the men strove to re-pitch the fallen tents. We started to secure the few loose articles around us; we looked for our blanket, but it was gone, with the thatch, and several minor articles that were no more to be seen. The men lay close under the fallen fluttering tents, whilst I and my trembling companion found shelter in the lee of a rock, until morning roused every soldier to arms.

My wife, in the meantime, hastily collected a few of the scattered branches of the hut, and huddled them together, so as to cover an umbrella, which served as a ceiling to the thatchless roof, until I should return from duty and construct a more substantial dwelling.

Our loss, trifling as it may seem, was the more severely felt, as there was no opportunity of replacing it by any fair means of purchase. Our day's provisions were among the articles missing, and this was far from being a comfortable look out for the day, as I had to mount the advanced picquet that morning; however, we had a little money, and scarce as bread was it was to be had for a good price.

The advanced picquet was more than two miles from the camp, and as I had not taken any provision with me for the day, my wife bought a small loaf and a little wine; this last she mulled and mixed with some of the bread, and was bringing to me; but in her too great anxiety to reach me soon, by short roads, she slipped on one of the steep banks and rolled down a considerable declivity. Fortunately she was not hurt, but heartily vexed at her own mishap, returned to the camp, made a fresh purchase, and again hastened to me. The tear was in her eye as she related the misfortunes of the day, but she returned to camp gratified at having provided me with an unexpected and comfortable refreshment.

I speak not of these casualties as sufferings on my part, for there were many worse off than I; but I point them out as some of the privations to which the poor women following the army had to submit, and which many of them were ill able to endure, and received but little sympathy from their husbands while patiently bearing them.

On my return to camp, I set about constructing a hut that should be proof against wind and rain. One of my officers (Lieutenant D. Farquharson) very kindly made an offer of any pecuniary assistance I might require, and gave me a blanket to replace that which was lost. The latter I accepted gratefully, it was more than money could purchase, the former I declined, as I was far from being in want; but the offer, which I am certain was sincerely intended for my acceptance, impressed me with the most sincere regard for that officer.

I now became a complete Robinson Crusoe in my daily labour, when regimental duties permitted; and much I owe in gratitude to the memory of those who then superintended those duties, for the indulgent manner in which I was treated, and not being troubled with vexatious interruptions to draw me off from my domestic avocations. They are now no more; they have fallen on the battle-field of a foreign land. A few men willingly afforded me every assistance; their only recompense being a small drop of spirits, which my wife had carefully reserved from my daily allowance. The wood was at no great distance, and the face of the hills was covered with broad ferns, which served for thatch.

I now laboured hard for three days, and every spare hour, when off duty, was dedicated to the rendering of my hut proof against the weather. My friend Fraser gave me the use of the entrenching tools, and I dug an ample space within, three feet deep, and a trench around the outside, four feet deep; this was to carry off the water from the roof, and the latter I secured more substantially than many of our Highland *lothies* are in the north of Scotland, or than the *cabins* in the remote districts of Ireland. We were enjoying the comfort of its nightly shelter, and I was adding something daily towards its stability for upwards of two weeks; at last I constructed a fireplace under the roof, and one of the men had brought a bundle of sticks for fuel, and the fire was lighted for the first time.

I was sitting on my knapsack taking a late dinner, quite at home, with the dish on my knee, for I had no table, when the drum beat "Orders." I set down my dish (a wooden canteen, the one end of which was taken out) unfinished, attended the call, and with no small regret heard that the camp was to be struck, and everything ready to be moved off that night (the 9th November 1813). I cannot express how vexed I was to leave my little habitation, my sole property, which I held by military right; but I was bound to follow my feudal superior. I had reared it at the expense of a blister on every finger, and I exulted as much over it, in secret, as the rich man in the Gospel did over his extensive possessions and his plentiful stores.

On leaving the camp that night, many of the married people set fire to their huts, but I left mine with too much regret to become its incendiary; and my poor Mary shed tears as she looked back upon it, as a bower of happiness which she was leaving behind.

The moon shone in the- cloudless vault of heaven as we descended the narrow paths of the mountains; behind us were our camp-fires and blazing huts, while the ill-clothed and worse disciplined troops of Spain were hurrying up the mountain path to occupy the ground we had left. To our right appeared the enemy's watch-fires, blazing brightly on the distant brow of one of the diverging ridges that jut out from the main body of the Pyrenees, their picquets little dreaming that we were worming our way through the intricate windings so near their posts, in order to rouse them to work in the morning. On our left, a deep woody ravine, with its roaring stream, skirted our path; before us, the narrow ridge jutted out between two of those ravines, in a peninsular form, until its extremity overlooked the valley where we had witnessed the contest on the 6th of October. The path led us down by many a circuitous and steep descent to the vale of Urdach, which we reached by daybreak.

We were now approaching the Neville, and all its woody margins were lined with light troops, our battalions forming in columns about two furlongs from the bank of the river: not a musket was yet fired; there stood the brave but unfortunate soldiers of France; here stood a generous but unwelcome foe, ready to invade the sacred bounds of their loved country, and with this generous foe stood the implacable Portuguese and the equally vengeful Spaniards. France beheld us, in her threatened position, with the haughty look of defiance, and the stream, as yet unpolluted by the feet of the invaders, gave to the woods and rocks its rushing sound.

The earth trembled beneath the advancing tread of our columns. The guns were already posted on all the commanding eminences on the left of the river. The generals had given their orders regarding the attack about to be made, the movements likely to follow, and their *aids-de-camp* were flying from corps to corps with the preparatory directions; no voice was heard, save that of command, until the foot of the advanced skirmisher was dipped in the stream; the bullet arrests him in his advance, and, as if at the command of some necromancer, thick and obscuring clouds rise from bank to bank, from eminence to eminence, as the loud thunder of war bursts from ten thousand muskets.

The river is passed, and the soldiers of France retire or fall before their stern invaders. We pass through a wood and come to the bottom of a steep hill (the heights of Ainhoe), the face of which presents long ridges of formidable breastworks, behind which the enemy keeps up a heavy fire of musketry, and fears no danger in the security of his cover. On the summit, overlooking these works, is a battery which commands that part of the river within its range. The 11th regiment was now ordered to ascend and storm those breastworks, and never did a regiment perform a task so dangerous, so obstructed, and apparently impracticable, with better success or in better order; its line was preserved without a break, not only in climbing the hill, but in springing over the breastworks, bayoneting those that waited its approach, even until it cleared the battery on the western summit, where, justly proud of its conquest, it made the hills echo to its loud huzzahs.

Meantime our regiment advanced more to the right, where, on a gentle slope of the hill, stood the huts (the recent camp or quarters) of the enemy; some of those huts caught fire, and owing to the combustible material of which they were constructed, the whole were nearly enveloped in one blaze.

The position which the enemy had occupied in the morning was now in our possession, and the sixth division crowded the heights of Ainhoe.

While we had been thus engaged, that part of the enemy's forces which had watched our movements above Urdach, on perceiving the site of our late encampment occupied by the Spaniards, concluded that we had retired to winter-quarters, advanced upon them, and, although far inferior in number, drove them back to the heights above Mayo, where a sharp contest ensued, which ended in the defeat of the Spaniards, who fled down the mountain to the village. Here our hospital orderlies, convalescents, and stragglers, dressed in the respective uniforms of their different corps, turned out in something like military order, and weak and inefficient as they were, their presence stopped the career of victory to the arms of France, and the conquerors re-ascended the heights without being pursued, proud of having routed and dispersed four times their number; but by this time the clouds had disappeared, and afforded those victors an opportunity of seeing their own army defeated, and flying in their own native valleys, before those troops whom they considered as having retired to quarters.

There are many shifts in the game of war, and those writers, who give the history to future ages, will trace the causes and effects of each movement, and point out what the principal mover has anticipated. When a defeat is the result, how easy it is to show the causes that led to it; errors upon errors arise from every movement; but should victory crown the fortunate general, every disposition is laid down and measured off with mathematical precision and infallible results; if he break through the centre of the opposing army, though at the hazard of exposing both flanks of his own, and success crown his efforts, it will be recorded as a masterly manoeuvre. Should he attempt to turn the right, at the risk of his own centre and left, succeed in so doing, and gain the day, he will be marked down as the Wellington or Napoleon of the age.

But in pursuing any of those plans, should a reverse occur, all are ready to point out every error; how it might and ought to have been foreseen, and averted or remedied; where advantages might have been taken, and where they were neglected. It is, therefore, not much to be wondered at, that a soldier thinks less about the points of attack than he does of the vigour with which they should be attacked, and of the leader's abilities to push forward, so as to hold fortune fast when within his grasp.

It may be questioned what would have been the result, had the enemy known what was passing on the banks of the Neville, and been able to pursue the panic-struck Spaniards past Mayo, or retrograded on the road leading through the pass to Urdach, and fallen on the rear of our army. Fortunately, he was not sufficiently strong to attempt the latter, and wanted confidence to pursue the other, so as to give any serious alarm; and, perhaps, no writer takes notice of this part of the action, so disgraceful to Spain, yet so honourable to France. The regiment's loss this day did not exceed twenty-seven killed and wounded; among the latter were Captain Mungo M'Pherson and Lieutenant Kenneth M'Dougall.

This was the first engagement I was in, and I considered myself no longer a recruit. I had now smelled the enemy's powder, as the old soldiers boastingly exclaimed; I had heard his bullets whistling past my ears, seen them dropping harmless at my feet, and burrowing in the ground.

I had observed, during this contest, the men whom I knew to be the greatest boasters in the company, men who never ceased enlarging on the exploits they had accomplished, the actions they had witnessed, or the hardships they had endured, when they had such a one as myself to listen to their stories; I observed some of those boasters very closely, and I could not help remarking, that the men who spoke less acted better.

It is perhaps needless to observe, that it is scarcely in the power of an individual foot soldier to perform any enterprising feat in the field of action, unless he be on some detached duty in front, such as is frequently the case with the skirmishers. If he is with the battalion, he must keep in his ranks; it is on the united movement of the whole body that general success depends; and he that rushes forward is equally blameable with him who lags behind, though certainly the former may do so with less chance of censure, and no dread of shame. A man may drop behind in the field, but this is a dreadful risk to his reputation, and even attended with immediate personal danger, while within the range of shot and shells: and woe to the man that does it, whether through fatigue, sudden sickness, or fear; let him seek death, and welcome it from the hand of a foe, rather than give room for any surmise respecting his courage; for when others are boasting of what they have seen, suffered, or performed, he must remain in silent mortification. If he chances to speak, some boaster cuts him short; and, even when he is not alluded to, he becomes so sensitively alive to these merited or unmerited insults, that he considers every word, sign, or gesture, pointed at him, and he is miserable among his comrades.

I have seen it frequently remarked, in the periodicals of the time, that the loss in killed and wounded was greater than was actually acknowledged on our side; that we overrated the enemy's loss, and underrated our own; but this is not the case.

The loss of the enemy, of course, is a guess rather than a certainty, until we become possessed of their official returns; but that of our own is never underrated. Indeed, a soldier feels a greater pride in boasting of his wounds than in trying to conceal them; mere scratches are often magnified into wounds, and stated as such in the returns.

There formerly existed a fund from which a reward was given to those whose blood was drawn in the field. This originated, no doubt, through some patriotic motive of the founders; yet the consequences of such a premium were certainly not well considered.

I never yet, among the many I have seen wounded, knew but one individual who kept his wound from being placed on the list; his name was Stewart. We were evacuating a redoubt on the heights of Toulouse, when a bullet struck him behind, pierced through his cartridge-box, cut his clothes, and hit him smartly on the breech.

"I shall give that to the rascal again," he said, as he recovered himself and picked up the bullet. "I shall be ashamed," he added, " to let it be known that I was struck behind."

Had this bullet struck him on the breast or limbs, there would have been one more on our list of that day's casualties.

It is not in one's power to give correct returns of the casualties on the night after an action; some are returned missing who have been killed; others returned killed who may have been severely wounded, and left apparently lifeless behind, yet may recover; they fall on the field where our feet never again passes; as the reapers in harvest drive on and leave the sheaves for others to gather up, so we advance and leave the fallen for others to raise.

Although the action at passing the Neville may not be considered of great importance, yet it ought to be a day of proud remembrance to the 11th regiment, not only on account of the success with which its efforts were crowned in the view of all the corps composing the division, but owing to the exemplary manner in which each man conducted himself, no one stooping to snatch a paltry booty from a fallen foe, and thus occasion a break in the ranks. Indeed, the manner in which it conducted itself on that day, might have served as a lesson to every corps that witnessed its movements, in showing how far good discipline tends to secure victory.

We bivouacked on the field until morning, and fortunately for us the night was fair, though cold and frosty.

This was the first night on which my wife and I had to lie down with no other covering than a blanket between us and the sky, but we had many worse nights than this afterwards, and worse fields before us; however, on looking around, we generally saw many worse off than ourselves; and, doubtless, were we always to look into others' misfortunes or sufferings, when we suffer ourselves, we would find some cause for self-congratulation amidst the most distressing hardships.

As soon as the position was taken up by the troops for the night, the culinary operations commenced; and not a few of the lovers of enterprise stole off, on purpose to cater some extra provisions for the mess, or search for other spoil, no less desirable because it was hazardous.

This manner of unwarrantably furnishing themselves by stealth, is justly termed *marauding* by our official authorities; if the act be attended by violence, it is called *rapine;* but, on purpose to divest it of either of these offensive appellations, the soldiers call it *reconnoitring;* thus softening it down to a more honourable undertaking, in the military phrase, so as to justify, in their own opinion, their nocturnal excursions for booty.

Those who proceeded on these forbidden enterprises stole off clandestinely from the camp or quarters by night, or cunningly contrived to join some of the wood or watering parties sent out from the camp, and then, evading the vigilance of the officer in command, slipped off unobserved on their private adventure, to the houses in which none of the military were quartered. They were frequently, too, made very welcome at the houses in which troops were quartered: the presence of men of another corps visiting there, without any known purpose, save that of looking for wood or water, gave a scope to the possessors to help themselves to what they could lay their hands upon, and throw the blame on the strangers.

The provisions, thus unwarrantably procured, were better and more highly appreciated than those served out by the commissary, and more anxiously looked for; yet, although they had been worse than those with which we were regularly supplied, there was something in the adventure which the men seemed very much to covet; whether it was to glory in the risk which they ran of being detected, and at the same time avoiding discovery, or that "Stolen waters are sweet, and bread eaten in secret is pleasant," therefore more to be prized than that which they daily received, may be doubtful; they certainly, however, preferred the hazardous means of obtaining it.

In the neighbourhood of our bivouac was a small hamlet or village, in which some of those stragglers, by carelessness or accident, set one of the houses on fire. In an instant the flames became a beacon over the face of the country, while the screams of distress and the shouts of mirth were wafted by the night-breeze from the ill-fated place, giving a sad lesson to the unfortunate inhabitants that were not yet visited by our arms.

Orders had been issued, previously to our entering France, to guard against any irregularities in the neighbourhood of our camps or cantonments, or of offering any violence to the inhabitants; and the commanding officers of corps were now again called upon, by the commander of the army, to enforce a strict compliance with these orders; and in order the more effectually to confine the men to their camp, the rolls of companies were called hourly both by day and by night. This was a very harassing system, but it tended not a little to prevent plundering.

During the time we were encamped on the Pyrenees, overlooking France, the country appeared as an extensive plain seemingly blessed with eternal sunshine; whilst, wrapped in clouds, whole days passed off with us in drizzly darkness, nor opened one gladdening chink through which we might view the charming scene. How anxiously we then wished to tread this sunny land of which we sometimes only caught a casual glimpse, and like a promised paradise, mocked us only with a distant prospect. We had now obtained our ardent wish, though at the expense of leaving some little attachment behind; but we were far from finding the fields so pleasant or the skies so cloudless as we had anticipated. No level plain as yet appeared in view; but hills and dales, broken roads, and rapid streams without bridges, and many a miry field, impeded our lagging march.

With torn shoes and lacerated feet, we advanced, on the 11th November, under a heavy fall of hail and snow, the first of winter's stormy blasts which threatened to obstruct our progress. Night brought us to a wood which afforded a little shelter and plenty of fuel for our fires, where, until morning, we stretched ourselves round the welcome blaze.

On the 12th we continued our march, though very slowly, being delayed by frequent halts, occasioned by the obstacles thrown in the way of our advance by the enemy, who were making good their retreat to the Nive.

The smaller streams were now swollen to rivers, and all the fields were completely swamped, yet we had to encamp, and fortunate were they who found shelter under the canvas.

In the vicinity of the camp was an eminence thickly sprinkled with tall furze bushes, and under the inviting shade of these our married people found a tolerable shelter, by clearing round the bottom and inclining the tops inwardly, so as to form an arch, over which a blanket was spread, and thus formed a hut with little labour and no expense.

It is not a little conducive to our health, as well as to our comfort, to have pointed out to us the manner in which our domestic wants may be supplied by a little labour; and when ourselves are the individuals benefited, we put our hands the more willingly to the work—work, which gives strength to our limbs and vigour to the body, banishes every lagging humour that may be gathering to clog the springs which keep the animal mechanism in motion, and at the same time banishes melancholy and discontent.

After remaining three days in this place, which we termed, "the wet camp," the whole army were ordered into cantonments.

CHAPTER 7

Fighting Our Way to Bayonne

The sixth division of the army was commanded by Major-General Sir Henry Clinton, and was cantoned in the town and neighbourhood of Ustritz, on the left bank of the Nive. It was composed of three brigades—the right, left, and centre. The first, usually termed the Highland Brigade, was commanded by Major-General Sir Denis Pack, and consisted of the 42nd (Royal Highlanders), the 79th (Cameron Highlanders), the 91st (Argyle Highlanders), and one company of the 60th (Royal Rifle Corps). The 11th, 32nd, 36th, and 61st regiments composed the left brigade, under the command of Major-General Sir John Lambert. The centre brigade consisted of three regiments of Portuguese, under the command of Colonel Douglas.

Having taken up our quarters, after a long and fatiguing campaign, the soldiers expected to be indulged in that ease, the enjoyment of which is as fondly courted by them as by the peaceful shepherd; but our generals, anticipating the fatal consequences resulting to armies by a sudden relaxation from field duties to sheltered idleness, found means to avert the danger by keeping us constantly employed by day, always ready by night, and at our alarm posts every morning before daybreak.

We had little chance, however, of becoming enervated by indulging ourselves in luxuries to which we had been long strangers, as the inhabitants had retired on our approach and left nothing behind worth taking. We had therefore to depend upon our daily allowance of provisions, which was limited to one pound of ship-biscuit, one pound of beef, and one-third of a pint of spirits. We received occasionally a little rice; but this was a gratuity to which we had no just claim, consequently not regularly issued. Had these articles been good, the quantity might have been sufficient, but the biscuit was frequently crushed to crumbs or mouldered to dust, and the beef would not have been allowed a stall in the poorest market of Great Britain. The spirits were generally good, and when mixed with a little toasted biscuit, proved an exhilarating breakfast.

We were frequently blaming the commissariat for the bad quality of our provisions; but if we had taken into consideration the innumerable difficulties with which it had to contend in procuring them, the obstacles that were to be surmounted in forwarding them to their respective depots, and then the thousand impositions* practised on the commissariat by small parties and detachments, it was really astonishing how it existed; and perhaps, on the whole, no army similarly situated was ever so well supplied as we then were.

---

* Parties were frequently proceeding from one place to another on various duties, and at the close of the day's march they received the following day's rations, on applying at the commissary store, and producing a check from that where the last issue was made. These were frequently forged in duplicate, the provisions drawn on the real check at night, and another of the same party, next morning, drew on the forged duplicate, when the multiplicity of business and the pressing for dispatch allowed no time to detect these frauds. Thus every day some cunning soldiers contrived to have two rations. These impositions, viewed in the abstract, were no doubt criminal, but under the circumstances in some degree pardonable; they could not be committed by any other than small parties on the march to or from their respective headquarters, and I never heard of any being detected. The men were marching without a farthing in their possession to purchase a mouthful of bread, even if it could have been pot for money; and is there any stout healthy man but will think the whole day's allowance too little for two meals, en a march of twenty miles or more? And every soldier knows that England would denounce the pusillanimous commissary through whose means one of her soldiers would perish for want of a sufficient supply.

At that time salt was a most desirable article, much in request, and not to be got at any price where we were cantoned. This scarcity was owing to the inhabitants having carried off or secreted every culinary article, leaving little behind but bare fields and empty houses. At the same time our advance into France excited hopes of obtaining plenty of every thing of which we were in want. "When we were encamped on the mountains, and looking down through some opening of the clouds to this land of promise, it was pointed out as the abundant repository from which all our wants were to be supplied, and was jocosely called "The place of all sorts." These anticipations, together with the certainty of approaching nearer the coast, made us less provident than under less flattering anticipations we would have been, and the last grain of salt had disappeared, even from the table of our colonel, before a party was dispatched to St. Jean de Luz in order to purchase a supply.

The roads were at that time like the miry bottoms of neglected trenches, into which stones had been cast to afford a foot passenger the means of stepping over; and notwithstanding the utmost anxiety of the party to proceed, the sun had set before it reached St. Pié. This was a circuitous route, but the muleteers by whom it was accompanied were its guides, and they were of opinion that the more direct road was impassable, or partly in possession of the enemy. The regiment, however, had the satisfaction of seeing the party return on the third day after its departure, with a sufficient supply of the desired article. Thus one of our pressing wants was removed, but several other cravings remained to exercise the ingenuity of the necessitous in finding means to gratify them.

It may appear incredible to some, that notwithstanding the express inhibition of the Articles of War then in force, a number of soldiers attempted to traffic with the enemy's sentries. This was not a little interrupted on our taking up our cantonments at Ustritz, in consequence of the river, which formed the line of separation, being much swollen by the late rains; and the French sentries, chiefly young conscripts, being unacquainted with the Portuguese language, which was generally understood by the old campaigners of both armies. In hazarding an enterprise of this kind, one of our men was detected in attempting to cross the river, and was supposed to be about to desert, brought back, tried by a general court-martial, and sentenced to death; and this sentence would have been carried into effect, had not the testimony of the surgeon gone to prove that the man was subject to fits of mental aberration, in consequence of a wound received in action. Indeed the attempt seemed more like that of one in a fit of inebriety than of a sober person, as the river was not fordable, and he was encumbered with several canteens strapped over his shoulders, a plain indication of the object of his pursuit.

On the night of the 8th of December our division was under arms in columns of brigades until nearly daybreak, the artificers being employed in placing a bridge of pontoons over the river, below the town. As soon as this was finished the troops began to pass along, while the drummers, left behind, beat the reveille at the usual places. This circumstance induced the enemy to conclude that we still occupied our quarters, although we were forming our columns silently in their neighbourhood, concealed amidst a dense mist. As soon as objects were discernible, a signal gun announced our time of advance. A wooden bridge still remained over the river at Ustritz, but so far broken down by the enemy as to be impassable; the discharge of this gun, however, so alarmed the French conscript sentries posted at the end of the bridge, on the right bank, that they retired in great haste towards the picquet to which they belonged, and our artificers lost no time in making the necessary repairs for the passage of the troops and stores.

The greater part of this day's action consisted in skirmishing, in which the light-infantry companies sustained the principal brunt. Towards the close of the day, the enemy retired upon a farm-house situated on a commanding eminence, having some of the adjoining fields enclosed by low dry-stone walls and quickset hedges, behind which they appeared in considerable force, supported by some artillery. In dislodging these troops, Captain George Stewart and Lieutenant James Stewart, both of the light company, were killed on the spot, and Lieutenant Brander was severely wounded.

Connected by kindred ties, the two former, whose loss we had to deplore, associated together, while in life, as brothers: as their pursuits were the same, so were the distinguished features in their characters. In the performance of their duty, and in every manly virtue, they seemed to be actuated by the same spirit. Complaisant and condescending, without meanness; strict, without severity; and brave, without presumptuous daring; one tent covered them in camp, and one table witnessed their little festivities in quarters; in the field they fought together, and one grave, consecrated by their blood, received their last remains; the peal of battle rung over their grave, and the funeral volleys conveyed to their enemies the messengers of death, and were those of vengeance. Here the two friends lie interred; a soldier's blanket is their shroud; no sculptured stone marks the spot or records their name, but it is impressed on our remembrance, from which death only can efface it.

I regret to say, that an outrage, revolting to the feelings of a generous soldier, was said to have been committed on the person of one of the family who had the misfortune to be beleaguered in the farm-house round which the contest raged. Indeed, violence was so seldom heard of, that the man who acted upon that principle, beyond the authorised custom of war, was distrusted by those who were led in to be participators, and detested by the better disposed, who refused to become associates in his guilt.

Rapine or pillage, though generally considered as a concomitant of war, is seldom allowed to be in accordance with the character or pursuit of a British soldier. It is equally as much in opposition to the high-mindedness of the brave as it is in accordance with the meanness of the avaricious ruffian; and although circumstances of necessity may palliate at times the offence of soldiers helping themselves to provisions in an enemy's country, yet neither time nor circumstances can justify wanton cruelty, or the indulgence of desires which humanity forbids, on the terrified females, who, neglectful of their own safety, cling to the protecting arms of their parents, and hazard their lives in the approaching storm of battle, rather than abandon them.

The individual, whose violence has drawn forth these remarks, was made prisoner by the enemy about three months after this occurrence, as he was on a marauding excursion in the neighbourhood of Pau; he was returned as a deserter, and on his afterwards joining the regiment at Auch, he received the punishment for desertion which he so richly deserved for rape.

Our casualties in this day's action were only eleven men, besides the officers already named. We bivouacked as usual during the night after an engagement, and a thousand fires soon lighted the field of our labour and our repose.

In the neighbourhood of our bivouac were a few straggling houses, in which some staff officers took up their quarters, and our guard was posted under the leafless branches of a chestnut tree, in the close vicinity. The sergeant of our guard being a married man, considered himself very fortunate in having secured a small pigsty near his post, for his wife's accommodation, and the poor woman felt happy in the possession, small as it was; for its roof was a shelter from the wintry blasts, and its contiguity to the guard left no room to fear danger, were she permitted to keep possession; however, this was not to be the case.

Our adjutant's clerk, who had never occasion to approach the field in time of danger, had taken up his quarters in one of the adjoining houses, after the action ceased, but being dispossessed by some superiors, and every other place preoccupied by soldiers who would not suffer his intrusion, he meanly invaded the miserable shelter selected for the poor woman.

In vain she remonstrated with him, in vain she requested him with tears to allow her the sole possession of a place so unfit for his accommodation, and which she had laboured hard to clean out for her own; but to no purpose, she might remain if she pleased, but he should not depart.

It is doubtful whether we had a woman in the regiment so regardless of her character as to have taken a night's shelter in the absence of her husband, otherwise than with the crowd, where no advantage could be taken of her situation or weakness; but every man acted towards a modest woman with that kindness which he would towards a sister. Indeed, we had women in the regiment, that if they had been in possession, would have kept him out, and put him at defiance to enter, but this one was not possessed of that masculine boldness; she, therefore, bundled up her few articles, and hastening across the road, the only distance by which she had been separated from her husband, threw herself into his arms and burst into tears.

Three months only had elapsed since this couple joined the regiment. She was a comely, modest, interesting young woman, and always unassumingly hut cleanly and decently dressed. But allowing that she had had but few or no accomplishments or amiable qualifications to recommend her to sympathy, it is but natural to think that whatever distressed her affected the husband. They had as yet seen or experienced but little of the petulant intrusions or consequential presumptuous ill-manners to which soldiers and their wives are sometimes obliged to submit without remonstrance.

"What is the matter with you, dear?" the sergeant asked, somewhat astonished at her unexpected appearance; for by the kindly appellation of *my dear* he usually addressed his wife. "Oh!" she exclaimed, "I've been turned out o' yon bit placey that I was in, an' I'm come to stop wi' you a' night."

"Who turned you out?" the sergeant hastily inquired.

"Oh, say naething about it, I'll be as well here wi' you as I would ha'e been yonder by mysel'; let us mak' no disagreement about the matter, wi' them that we canna shake oursel's free o'; let the proud little creature keep it to himsel' in quietness; we are strangers as yet, so dinna let angry words be heard."

"But what creature turned you out? Surely it was not a man."

"Ay, he thinks himsel' ane;" she whispered, "It was G—t."

"Is it possible," said the Sergeant, "that a married man can be possessed of so little feeling as to turn you out to the inclemency of the night, and neither his wife nor child accompanying him to plead for the accommodation? But let him keep it," he continued, as he spread his blanket over her shoulders, "my blanket can cover us both; his favour I ask not, and his malice I put at defiance. The man who is capable of acting so ungenerously to a woman can never prosper or be deserving of the good opinion of a soldier, and I should be sorry to court or even accept the kindness or friendship of such a man."

"I am happier with you," she replied, "than if I had lain all night in yon hole; but, dear, O dear, how hard it rains; the fire will be drown'd out, an' we'll be starved to death before mornin'."

"Poor body!" the sergeant ejaculated, as he wrapped the blanket round her shoulders, "I'll soon make a good fire, sit you under that branch of the tree, the *reek* will annoy you less, and the drops will not fall so thick nor so heavy."

"I'm well enough," she returned, "and I care na' for the *reek* or the rain when wi' you; but dinna min' the fire till this heavy dag's o'er; ye'll get yoursel' a' wet."

The sergeant threw a faggot of wood on the fire, and in a short time nothing was heard but the rattling of rain and hail-stones, the braying of mules, and the tinkling of their bells.

This was a severe night, the rain poured down in torrents until midnight, when it was succeeded by snow, which covered the face of the country before daybreak.

The sudden change of the weather occasioned the sixth

division being ordered back to reoccupy its former quarters, whilst the second, under the command of Sir Rowland Hill (now Lord Hill), took up cantonments from Villafranque, to which village we had advanced, to the eastward, as far as Vieux Moguere, on the right of the main road from St. Jean Pied-de-Port to Bayonne, with its rear resting on the right bank of the Nive.

We were not a little disappointed, on our return to Ustritz, to find that the owners had taken possession of our quarters, during our two days' absence, and considered us rather unwelcome guests. This was not to be wondered at, for they had, very likely, been suffering great privations from the time we had taken possession and, doubtless, they found things in a very different state from that in which they had left them.

We were now obliged to rest satisfied with less accommodation than we had had, and this was confined to the worst, the meanest, and filthiest places, which we had to put in order for ourselves. Instead of a small parlour which we had occupied, with a few more, we were glad to get as much room as to spread a blanket upon the floor under a stair.

Our time of occupation, however, was but short; the calm produced by the change of the weather was only that which precedes the tempest. Marshal Soult, possessed of every advantage for the movement of his troops, having Bayonne with its navigable communications upon the Adour open in his rear, availed himself of the interruption which was given by the state of the roads to our advance, to draw off the greater part of his army, during the night of the 9th, to his right. This was easily accomplished, by making it retire on the main road leading from Pied-de-Port to Bayonne, thence advancing on that leading to St. Jean de Luz.

These roads were always good, and the connecting link or key, namely, Bayonne, solely in his possession, while all the cross roads by which our troops had to move from flank to flank were almost impassable, and crossed by deep torrents, the bridges over which had been damaged or destroyed.

During the 10th and 11th, the marshal pressed with all his force against the left of our army, which was posted on both sides of the Jean de Luz road, but, being repeatedly repulsed, he retrograded on the night of the 12th and pushed towards his left, where the contest had been broken off on the evening of the 9th. By this movement, his force on the road to Pied–de–Port is said to have amounted to thirty thousand; to oppose which General Hill had not more than thirteen thousand, including our division, cantoned, as I have already observed, on the left bank of the Nive, in his rear; and Sir L. Cole's and a brigade of the third division from the left, where they had been engaged or in movement the two preceding days.

Soult had anticipated, that by his pressing attack on our left, for two days successively, he should have obliged Lord Wellington to withdraw the principal part of his force from the right, and so weaken that flank as to enable him to over-power it; but this was foreseen by our great commander, and we were on the march, early on the morning of the 13th, towards the Adour.

The weather had been rather favourable during the two preceding days; a hard frost bound up the miry face of the country, and enabled us to advance with considerable speed during the morning, but as the day advanced, we were im-peded by the cloggy and adhesive soil of the fields, and the sun had gained the meridian before we cleared the valley westward of Villafranque, and ascended the partially wooded heights that afford a distant view of Bayonne and the Adour to the north, of Jean de Luz and the Bay of Biscay to the west, of the windings of the Nive, of the white villages and hamlets on its green banks, and of the snow-covered Pyrenees beyond, that seemed to rise in a perpendicular ridge to the clouds, bounding the view in our rear.

On our right, the face of the country presented a broken, moorland, hilly aspect, and was apparently in the progress of being reclaimed and *feued* out for cottages; several were half finished, and the material for others laid down. The main road from Bayonne to Pied-de-Port runs along the west side or end of a hill bounding the view to the east.

During the time of our advance, the attack had been made by the enemy; he had so far established himself on the main road as to have Villafranque upon his right; this village is situated on a height, and is about two miles from the road, with a marshy valley between them.

On the sixth division's attaining the heights overlooking Bayonne, its movements were immediately directed to its right, so as to support more effectually the left of the second; and Sir Denis Pack ordered the 42nd to advance to the main road, by which a brigade of the enemy was retiring. Our colonel was as anxious to execute the order as the men were proud to have been selected to perform it, but he led us into such a brake of furze, thorns, and brambles, that it would have been impossible to have taken our bare thighed regiment through its impenetrable meshes. The general, observing our painful but ineffectual struggling, withdrew us from that spot, and pointed to another place by which we should have advanced, and which would have been practicable; but by this time the enemy had passed our mark, and were descending towards the valley of the Adour, where, joined by another brigade, they made a determined stand against the 92nd (Highlanders), that were coming round on the other flank.

The ground at that place was intersected with deep drains, loose stone walls, and thorn bushes. Here a contest ensued, which cannot be described with justice to both parties; perhaps the like seldom or never occurred during the war. The enemy, although on their retreat, were within a short distance of their own fortified position of Bayonne, and in view of their own army and people, from whom praise or censure was to be expected; they were also in the animating discharge of an urgent duty, namely, that of opposing the invaders of their beloved country. Yet, notwithstanding all these stimulants, the gallant 92nd bore down every opposition. The guns ceased to play upon this spot, so closely were both parties intermixed.

Foe to foe grasped each other in mutual anger, and rolled together in the ditch. Muskets were broken, bayonets bent, and stones were thrown with deadly vengeance. Victory crowned our native band, but it was dearly bought. Fourteen officers, eight sergeants, and one hundred and sixty-three rank and file lay killed and wounded on the spot, and thrice that number of the enemy were scattered in heaps around them.

The sun sank over the blue waves of the Bay of Biscay, and darkness rested on the fields, before the fire of the skirmishers ceased. Both armies, wearied of the struggle, rested on the ground during the night, the picquets occupying the dilapidated remains of the houses in front: to these the wounded men crawled for shelter, or were carried thither, if near the spot; and it reflects a national credit on the men on duty, that the hand of kindness was equally extended towards the foe as to the friend.

Dry litter was obtained for their beds, every attention that one soldier could offer to another was bestowed, and in the morning, by order of Lord Wellington, the whole of the wounded of the enemy were carried into their own lines; and it certainly was gratifying to see those brave though disabled soldiers embracing those who had entertained them during the night, and kindly shaking the hand that perhaps inflicted the wound. Poor fellows! Many of them were young men, this perhaps their first appearance in arms to defend, in the true spirit of patriotism, the home of their fathers. Yes, perhaps even animated with a desire to re-establish the fallen fortunes of the great Napoleon, for still this name was dear to Frenchmen, and probably will be for ages to come.

The unfortunate men who had fallen in remote places were suffered to remain under the inclement sky, until morning brought them relief, or death ended their sufferings. The rain poured down heavily during the night, and those who had crawled for shelter to the dry ditches along the roads or fields, breathed their last beneath the gathering floods.

CHAPTER 8
The Battle of Orthez

The weather again put a stop to hostilities, and arrangements were made, without further delay, for the troops taking up winter-quarters. That part of the country assigned for our division, extended from Villafranque (the head-quarters of General Clinton) to the heights overlooking Bayonne, a district already overrun by both armies and stripped of every article of provision. The houses allotted for our accommodation were in a very dilapidated state, and the men were as much crowded in them as on board of transports.

The flooring of the lofts was so openly laid, that articles heavier than dust were frequently falling, either accidentally or designedly, for mischief or sport, on the head of some grumbling *wight* below. It was not a little owing to the generous disposition of our officers, confining themselves to less room than they might have done, if otherwise disposed, that our married people had generally an apartment assigned for themselves. In short, every class was so accustomed to the habits and usages of the campaign, that amidst every privation, each man made himself happy or apparently so.

At all the houses which we occupied, the fires were lit without the walls; parties were paraded by daybreak for the purpose of bringing wood for fuel, water for cooking, and also to go for provisions. The latter were issued at the commissary store; the wood and the water taken where it could be found.

Cooking was the most unpleasant duty which the men had to perform; green wood being the only fuel, it cast a cloud of smoke around the place, and while the rain threatened to extinguish the fire, the wind scattered the embers about, and almost prevented the most attentively persevering cook from finishing his task. It was not seldom that the meat, which was the poorest of the poor, was brought in little better than scalded, and this occasioned a grumble, but it was only a momentary one, some pleasant remark made all contented, and the luckless cook happy at having his task over.

Our mode of cooking was very simple, and the soup would have puzzled a Kitchener or Ude to give it a name; not a single blade of vegetable was to be had to put into it, our supply of rice was curtailed, and the only thickening for it was the crumbs and dust of the ship-biscuit. The lid of the camp-kettle served for a carving-dish, the cook's fingers supplied the place of a fork, and no symptom of delicacy or disgust appeared by any man's palate refusing or loathing the scanty morsel from those unclean fingers. No waste was to be observed; fortunately no half-starved dog stared us in the face imploring a bone, for it was a very hard one that was cast away without being completely denuded of meat, and its soft end gnawed sweetly. The commissariat butchers found ready purchasers for bullock's blood and offal, of which very good wholesome messes were made.

The nights passed off pleasantly in singing songs, and telling tales, until sleep overpowered all, and our dreams were of better times on our native shores. Every man lay down fully accoutred, as when on the campaign, and turned out before the beating of the reveille in the morning, each company at its alarm posts; and at that early hour the guards, picquets, working parties, &c. marched off to their respective posts of duty. Breastworks and batteries were constructed along the face of the heights looking towards Bayonne; and in the raising of these defences, we were employed during the time we remained in cantonments (from the 14th December to the 21st February following). During this time, the roads that intersected the country, between the two main ones so frequently mentioned, as leading to Bayonne, were almost impassable, being deeply covered with mire from side to side, while seldom a day passed over without rain, sleet, or snow.

A regular market was established at Villafranque, and although articles were extravagantly dear, yet they were to be got, which was considered no small advantage to those who had the money; and the utmost vigilance was used to protect the inhabitants, who were bringing supplies, from meeting with any interruption or insult from stragglers of the army.

A provost-marshal was stationed here, for the more effectually preventing offences and speedily punishing those who attempted to trespass. This functionary, though requisite for repressing delinquencies, is far from being in high repute in the army; his duty is the most unpleasant in the service, and perhaps in consequence of this, the one who holds it is generally rewarded, after the completion of his service as a provost, with the half-pay of a subaltern officer. During the time he is provost, he superintends the punishment of those sentenced by general courts-martial; he can also order any soldier or follower of the army punishment for marauding or other petty trespasses, when the delinquent is absent from the regiment to which he belongs; he can also punish a soldier for being absent from his regiment without leave, if found in any suspicious manner straggling. The punishment was inflicted on the spot, by the provost's drummer, upon the offender's breech. These punishments were pretty frequent, but as they were always inflicted on absentees, the corps to which the delinquent belonged was seldom apprised of the circumstance.

The immediate punishment of criminals, after being detected in trespassing on the confiding inhabitants of an invaded country, is certainly attended with better effect, in order to soothe the injured and to prevent crime, than the usual slow deliberations of courts-martial, notwithstanding that these are also considered quick in their proceedings. When the offended person sees, while the passion yet rages in his breast, the prompt manner in which the offenders are arraigned for trespassing on his person or property, and witnesses the ignominious punishment inflicted on those whom he so justly considers his enemies, it soothes his anger and reconciles him to the invaders, by convincing him that he is still to a certain extent protected.

We were paying, at this time, two shillings and sixpence for a loaf of bread between two and three pounds weight, termed a *Pampalonia;* the same price was asked for a pound of brown sugar; a pound of soap was the same price; and an English pint of milk was ten-pence, but that could rarely be obtained. Coffee and tea were scarce articles, and beyond the reach of a soldier's purse. We toasted the biscuit to serve as a substitute for coffee, and when a little wheat could be obtained it was preferred; we also considered wheat a very good mess, when boiled in water and left a few minutes to cool and swell.

I mention these circumstances merely that others may make the same or similar shifts, and be as well satisfied us we then were, when the time comes that they may be put to such trial, and no old campaigner with them to advise or direct. A soldier ought to feel a pride in the difficulties and privations that may come in his way, so that he may boast, if he loves boasting, of having overcome them. Wealth he may despise, since he cannot attain it, or if he attain, he may afterwards lose it; he may boast, however, of his perils, his privations, and of his poverty, and of these no one will defraud him; let him therefore never despair under misfortunes, but glorying in them, live in the anticipation of better times.

On the 21st of February the cantonments were broken up, and the campaign of 1814 commenced. Our march was directed by Hesperran, St. Palais, and Montford, on the Gave de Oleron.

On the afternoon of the 25th we were ordered to halt, just as we were about to ford the Gave, below a large farmhouse, where the river is fordable, but was said to have been set with spikes, so as to form an obstruction to our passage. Perhaps there was no truth in this report; however, we suddenly retrograded and passed on pontoons, not far from a small village, in which we were quartered for the night.

On the following day we approached the neighbourhood of Orthez, where we pitched camp on the south side of the gently rising heights, the north side of which forms the left bank of the Pau and overlooks the handsome town beyond. An explosion, occasioned by the blowing up of a bridge, excited the curiosity of a few to steal up the height, notwithstanding that we had been charged against discovering ourselves to the enemy; others followed the example, and as no measures were taken or perhaps were necessary to prevent it, the men indulged themselves with a view of Orthez, the beautiful valley, with the Pau stealing softly along its south side, while the long range of mountain heights bounding it on the north rose abruptly over the road leading from Bayonne and Peyrehorade. Many a man gazed on that mountain range, who little thought that before tomorrow's sun should go down, he would be stretched upon it a lifeless corpse. But these gloomy forebodings seldom intrude themselves on a soldier's mind; full of the anticipations of battle and victory, each man retired to his tent to enjoy a night's repose.

Such had been the general good and orderly conduct of the troops, during the few weeks we had been cantoned, that the inhabitants began to entertain a better feeling towards us than that with which they had been at first impressed on our invading their territory, and it was not a little satisfactory to find them keeping their houses and offering articles, for which they found amongst us ready purchasers and high prices; but this was necessary, in order to cover the frauds to which they were exposed, and which it was impossible to detect. It is not until the man who has committed the fraud is past the bounds of detection or prosecution, that he feels himself at liberty to boast of those unjustifiable transactions, and give them publicity among his companions.

Early on the morning of Sunday the 27th, we marched down the left bank of the Pau, passed on a pontoon bridge, and directed our course upon the main road up the valley towards Orthez. Two divisions of the army were already on the road before us. The heights on our left appeared to be in the possession of the enemy, and as our movements were plainly to attack his centre or his left, which was posted in and above the town, corresponding movements became necessary on his part, and his ranks were seen advancing along the ridge parallel with ours.

As the mountain approaches that place where the road to St. Severe passes over it from Orthez, there is a downward bend of about a mile; it rises, however, to a considerable height on the east side of that road, and commands the town and its approaches. On our coming near this bending, our brigade was ordered to move to its left; several enclosures were in our way, but this was no time to respect them, as the enemy was welcoming us with round shot and shell. The gardens and nurseries were trodden down in an instant, and a forest of bayonets glittered round a small farm-house that overlooked a wooded ravine on the north side.

The light companies, which had preceded the brigade, were keeping up a sharp fire upon the enemy's skirmishers, and our grenadier company was ordered to take post along the bank overlooking the ravine, and commanding a narrow road below. No place seemed less practicable for cavalry to act, but the enemy were determined to make every effort to re-establish their lines on the heights from which they had been driven by the light troops, and some of their squadrons were seen approaching to drive back our advance, which by this time was reinforced by the grenadiers; but the more effectually to repel an attack, two additional companies were dispatched to reinforce those already sent, and these had scarcely been formed when the charge of cavalry was announced: it was met and repulsed; men and horses were tumbled over the steep bank on the narrow road below, skirting the ravine.

The gallant young officer who led that charge, passed through the ranks like a lion pouncing on his prey, and was made prisoner by M'Namara of the grenadier company. This man, if my memory serve me well, gave the horse and sword to one of our captains, who was afterwards appointed brevet-major; but poor M'Namara, who was more of a soldier than a courtier, rose not to corporal; he is yet to be seen, not like the Sidonian whom the messengers of Alexander found weeding his garden when they sought him to be king, nor like the Roman cultivating his little-field, when he was requested to take the charge of an army, but employed in the humbler avocation of making wooden dishes, and occasionally selling them on the market street of Newry.

After this repulse of the cavalry, we passed through the ravine, and moved towards the road that passes over the bending of the hill. The light-infantry companies of the brigade, under the command of Major Cowel (afterwards brevet Lieutenant-Colonel), were skirmishing in front. The major was severely wounded and carried to the rear.

The hill rises rather abruptly on the east side of the road, and slopes gradually towards the north side, to which our advance was directed, in order to turn the enemy's right, which had fallen back as we advanced. The main road now defined the direct line between both armies; the enemy's left at Orthez, his centre on the south ascent to the summit of the hill, and his right from the summit descending to the fields on the north side.

There is a small village consisting of one street on that brow of the hill towards the north, upon which the enemy was driven back, and from this kept up a destructive fire of musketry from garden walls, windows, and loopholes. Our regiment was ordered to drive him from that annoying post, which I may say had now become the right of his position. The bearer of this order was Lieutenant Innes, who was then acting brigade-major to Sir D. Pack; he preceded the regiment, and may be said to have led it on. The word of command to advance at the charge, was received with loud animating cheers.

No movement in the field is made with greater confidence of success than that of the charge; it affords little time for thinking, while it creates a fearless excitement, and tends to give a fresh impulse to the blood of the advancing soldier, rouses his courage, strengthens every nerve, and drowns every fear of danger or of death, thus emboldened amidst the deafening shouts that anticipate victory, he rushes on and mingles with the flying foe.

In an instant the village was in our possession, and the fugitives were partly intercepted by the advance of the second division of the army, under Lord Hill, which had passed the Pau above Orthez, and was now approaching round the east end of the heights.

The enemy, thus dispossessed of his last position of any importance, commenced a hasty retreat through some enclosed fields and young plantations, through which his columns directed their course, until impeded by intersecting ditches which induced them to take the main road; there the ranks were broken, confusion ensued, and a complete route was the consequence.

Fortunately for them the sun was nearly set, and although the pursuit continued for several miles, they succeeded in keeping the lead; and having reassembled during the night, continued their retreat towards the Adour.

The loss of the regiment in this battle was four officers, six sergeants, and eighty-eight rank-and-file.

I have already mentioned that Lieutenant Innes (our adjutant) was doing the duty of brigade-major. It was near the close of this day's contest that he carried the orders of the general for the regiment to drive the enemy from the village situated on the north brow of the hill; he might have retired after delivering the orders, without throwing a blot on his good name, but his heart was with the regiment, and he advanced to the charge in person; not with a fearful heart or a half-shut eye, to watch the distant motions, but spurring forward his steed in the blazing front of battle, led the way to victory. It was amidst the animating shouts which arose around him, that the last hostile and fatal bullet pierced his brain, and laid him in the dust. He fell amidst our foremost ranks, and breathed his last between the saddle and the ground.

We left behind us our dead, our dying, and our wounded; the former careless who shut those eyes that looked up to heaven from their gory bed, or who should consign their naked limbs to a grave in the field of a strange land. But our dying are sometimes left to the mercy of strangers. Shall some good Samaritan bind up their wounds and afford them protection under some hospitable roof, in the country which their invading feet have trod, and while their hands are still reeking with the blood of its bravest defenders? Or shall some sanguinary wretch put an end to their life and pain at once? Perhaps this might be the most welcome to the toil-worn soldier; but, alas! a harder fate awaits many. The midnight plunderer shuts his ears to mercy's call, strips the helpless, bleeding, dying sufferer, and leaves him naked to breath his last beneath the frosty sky, on the field saturated with his blood.

Night suspended hostilities, and the army bivouacked in columns on the fields bordering the road leading to St. Severe.

Night, after a battle, is always glorious to the undisputed victors; they draw close to one another to hear and tell of the hazards of the day, while some show the petty prizes snatched off the field, and curse some intermeddling *satrap* that would not let them linger behind to get a better. The batmen and baggage-guard join the jocund circles round the camp fires, and exhibit some full canteens of wine, the hastily snatched spoil of the day, or the plunder of some poultry-house, baker's oven, or farmer's pantry, no less acceptable to men long used to mouldy ship-biscuit and scanty fare, than silver or gold would have been to those who experienced no want.

Midnight shuts our eyes in welcome slumber, and nought is heard to break the awful stillness that prevails, save the tinkling of the mule-bells and the tread of a silent soldier round the expiring embers of a camp fire.

On the 28th we advanced on the road leading to St. Severe, our cavalry in front, pursuing and harassing the enemy's rear, and making a number of his stragglers prisoners. Many of these were deeply gashed by sabre-wounds, and being unable to get on so fast as the escorts urged, they fell down by the roadside faint from loss of blood, or panting with thirst, frequently soliciting a little water to cool their parched tongues. It is but justice to say, that the British soldier attended to their appeals and relieved them, when in his power so to do, and sympathized as much for them as if they had never fired a shot at him.

In civil wars, the passions of the combatants may be mutually excited, by political causes or sectarian zeal, to deadly hatred; but with us no incentive but that of duty urged us on, and if our opponents at any time seemed actuated by a spirit of vengeance, it was not to be wondered at, as we were invaders.

We halted this day about three leagues from St. Severe, where the road is crossed by a considerable stream. A bridge had been destroyed here, and some trenches cut so as to impede the advance of our cavalry and guns. In consequence of these obstacles, we encamped on the south side of the valley looking towards a range of heights occupied by the enemy, and where we supposed a stand was to be made, and another battle the consequence, before we should be permitted to proceed much farther.

A considerable quantity of vine-supporters lay scattered in bundles contiguous to our regiment's camp-ground, and dry wood being always a desirable article for those who had the culinary duties to perform, a *general charge* was made, in order to secure a quantity, before the other regiments came to the knowledge of it.

Our colonel had just dismounted, and was about to proceed to a farmhouse adjoining to stable his horse, when the sudden rush of the men, after having piled their arms and thrown down their knapsacks, attracted his attention. He gazed upon them with astonishment, hesitated a moment, and asked one of the guard the cause of so sudden a movement: this soon discovered itself, for the men were loaded with armfuls of sticks, and rejoicing over their booty and good luck, anticipating the comfortable warmth it would afford during the drizzly night.

Sir Denis Pack had taken up his quarters in the farmhouse, or was supposed to have done so, and nothing was more likely than that he would take an interest in protecting the owner's property. The colonel, whether in dread of the general or a mistaken sense of justice, called out to the marauders, as he was pleased to call them, to carry back their burdens; some obeyed, others dropped them at their feet, and a few, less obedient, persisted in bringing them along; but the whole seemed rather unwilling to comply. The colonel, dissatisfied at the apathy displayed in obeying his orders, darted among the offenders, and personally chastised those who seemed the most reluctant to obey.

Among the most refractory of those wood foragers were two men of singular dispositions; their names were Henderson and Doury. The former was a contradictory, obstinate, careless, awkward fellow; his visage was long, his lips thick, his mouth always open, and, to use a Scotch term, *slavering*. His feet were flat-soled, without any spring, and he marched like a wearied peddler under a pack, jolting along the road; he had not seen much service, but, like many old soldiers, he had much to say; he was nicknamed "the Gomeral." Doury was a silly, good-natured simpleton, the butt of every man's jest, yet no jester himself; for, when excited, his utterance failed so far, that it was little else than a breathless gibbering of inarticulate sounds. Such another couple was not in the regiment, or perhaps in the brigade, and would not be accepted of for the service in time of peace.

Those two were bringing in their burdens, notwithstanding the interdiction, and had entered the field on which the colonel was standing. Ignorance could not be pleaded, for all the men had thrown down their loads at the colonel's desire, and had withdrawn, just as so many schoolboys would have done, from some forbidden ground, when their master's stern voice was heard. The colonel observing that Henderson led the other on, strode hastily forward to enforce obedience; Doury was the first to observe him, fled past his companion, dropped the sticks at his feet, and escaped. Not so Henderson; he fell over the bundle dropped at his feet, with his face pressed against the soft miry field; the colonel overtook him as he recovered, seized him by the kilt, the pins of which yielded to the tug, and left his naked posteriors to some merited chastisement. This excited bursts of laughter from all the men, and the poor fellow afterwards declared that he was more vexed at the laughter than hurt by the punishment.

Had the colonel been a severe or strict disciplinarian, or even a harsh commanding officer, he might have had recourse to courts-martial and punishments, after this display of opposition or reluctant obedience to his command; but no other punishment followed the offence than that which he had inflicted himself.

The interdiction imposed by the colonel on the regiment was of no small service to the men of the other corps, who failed not to benefit themselves by drawing their supplies of fuel without leave and without reprimand, from the same store from which we anticipated so much comfort.

War is considered a curse to any country engaged in it, but that which becomes the seat of it necessarily feels the scourge with more than tenfold violence. The victor may pour forth his hosts to fatten the fields of a foreign land, and his loss be scarcely reckoned amongst the millions of his nation, though the tidings may give sorrow to individuals whose friends have fallen in battle. Though the mother may bewail the loss of her son. the wife that of her husband, the sister of a brother, or the maid that of her lover; yet she sees not the hand of oppression by which the vanquished are held down, neither does she hear the tread of the unwelcome invader approaching her dwelling; her hearth is inviolate; no marauder steps in to claim a superior right to its comforts; no prowling straggler from a hostile camp preys upon her property, searching for booty, as is the case where adverse armies are assembled.

Notwithstanding the frequent roll-calls to keep the men from marauding, plenty flowed into the camp through illicit channels during the night, evading guards, picquets, patrols, and sentries.

It may be asked, "Were not the officers and non-commissioned officers very remiss in their duty, in not suppressing those unwarrantable oppressions, so manifestly opposed to the orders of the commander of the forces? Was not the acceptance of any part or portion of the booty (for we must believe that part of it fell to the officers or non-commissioned officers' share) a participation in the violence offered to the inhabitants? Was not the overlooking of those breaches of orders on the part of the plunderers, equivalent to a silent assent to their actions?"

He that questions thus, may do so from the best of motives, namely, philanthropy; but soldiers are not philanthropists; and the questioner would perhaps be inclined to relax a little from the laudable principle which may actuate his conduct and feelings when sitting comfortably at home, were he placed under similar circumstances, in a hostile country, after months of half-fasting and half-feeding on bare bones and mouldy ship-biscuit; and I assure him, that the officers' share of those things was less than some may imagine. Yet the pleasure of occasionally seeing plenty and cheerfulness around, gave them a satisfaction surpassing that which they could have had, if they had been inquisitively pressing to know whence every mouthful of meat came into the soldier's possession.

CHAPTER 9

The Battle of Toulouse

On the 1st of March we passed St. Severe, and forded the Adour about a furlong below the bridge, which the enemy had been endeavouring to break down, but had not thoroughly succeeded in their attempt; they had damaged it so far, however, as to retard the advance of our guns until the breach was repaired.

The river at this place seems little inferior to the Shannon at Limerick, but the stream spreads more equally over the channel, no part being deeper than three feet at the ford. In passing through, the men supported each other as well as they could, so as to prevent them falling, for the stones in the bottom were very slippery.

The wife of a sergeant of one of the regiments attempted to pass on a donkey, with a child in her arms, and owing to some sudden stumble or slip of the animal, the child gave a start and dropped into the stream; the distracted mother gave a shriek, leaped after the infant, and both were swept off by the rapid current, in the presence of the husband, who plunged into the water in hopes to recover them, but they were gone for ever, and he himself was with difficulty rescued.

After this accident, the women who were following the army remained until the bridge was so far repaired as to enable them to pass over.

After having crossed the river, we marched a few miles up the right bank, or contiguous thereto, on the main road, and took up our camp-ground for the night in a newly ploughed field, rendered a complete mire by the rain and hail which fell upon us with dreadful fury as we were piling our arms on the broken ridges. Yet, notwithstanding the severity of this headlong torrent, a hundred fires were blazing in a few minutes along the side of the fences that bordered the fields. Fortunately for us, General Pack had taken up his quarters in the farmhouse adjoining, and allowed straw, of which there was abundance, to be taken for the bottom of the tents; this was an unexpected indulgence, even although the straw was rather wet.

I was General Pack's orderly this night, and had a good roof over my head, and the dry floor of a cart-shed, with plenty of dry straw for a bed; but my poor wife was absent, for the first time since we left home. She was detained along with several other women, on the right bank of the Adour, until the bridge was repaired. While this was doing, one of the women belonging to the regiment begged her to take charge of a little ass-colt with a couple of bundles, until she should go back to St. Severe to make some purchases; she complied, and before the other returned, the bridge was repaired. One regiment had passed, and she followed, driving the colt before her; but before she got to the further end, the stubborn animal stood still and would not move a foot.

Another regiment was advancing, the passage was impeded, and what to do she knew not. She was in the act of removing the woman's bundles from the beast's back, and struggling to get out of the way, determined to leave the animal, when a grenadier of the advancing regiment, casting his eye on a finely polished horn with the Masonic arms cut on it, and slung over her shoulder, stepped aside, saying:

"Poor creature, I shall not see you left struggling there, for the sake of what is slung by your side."

At the same time handing his musket to one of his comrades, he lifted the colt in his arms and carried it to the end of the bridge. My poor wife thanked him with the tear in her eye, the only acknowledgment she could make for his kindness; but she has often thought of it since, and congratulated herself on having the good fortune to have that horn, empty as it was, with its talismanic hieroglyphics, slung by her side, on that occasion, and thus to raise up a friend when she was so much in need of one.

There was a corporal's guard over the general's quarters, and in the morning we had an excellent fire in front of the house, where a few of the men from the camp came to warm themselves and dry their clothes and appointments; among these were the adjutant's clerk, some of the guard, and myself.

During this time one of the guard, unaccompanied by the corporal, relieved the sentry, and posted himself, without the ceremony of regular relief. This was done, if not to our knowledge, at least where we might have seen it; but, indeed, this mode of relieving was so common, when it could pass without detection, that the non-commissioned officers, as well as the privates, did not think much about it, notwithstanding its being a very serious breach of duty. The general had observed the whole proceeding from his window, which overlooked the place, and lost no time in repairing to the spot. He commenced by interrogating the clerk on the subject, and he denied having observed it; this put the general in a passion, for he had doubtless observed very well how far we were culpable before he came to question about the matter.

"As for you," said Sir Denis, turning to me, "you are no less guilty than he, to be standing there without attending to what is passing; go instantly," he continued, "and confine those two men, report to Colonel Macara having done so, and also that two of his own sergeants were present when the breach of duty for which the sentries are confined was committed, and without offering the least opposition to it. I shall leave it to the colonel to take such steps as he may think fit to put a stop to such irregularities."

It was certainly very lenient in the general, to allow me to be the reporter of my own negligence; for if he had had an intention to visit our neglect or oversight with more than a reprimand, he would have sent another messenger or a written communication to the colonel, and not a verbal message by one of those concerned in the matter of complaint, one who was to be considered guilty, and would not fail to make the report as favourable for himself as possible. However, I make little doubt but the general thought he had inflicted considerable punishment by his own personal reprimand.

In proceeding to execute my disagreeable commission, I met the colonel on his way to the general's, and began to state the message with which I was charged.

"Two of the men," I said, "are confined by order of the general, for relieving and posting irregularly; it has been done without the corporal's knowledge, but as I am the general's orderly for the day, and was on the spot, most likely the men thought there was no harm in relieving as I was standing beside them."

The colonel interrupted me by saying, "There is always something disagreeable occurring to the general's notice, very unpleasant indeed; but here he comes himself."

After passing the usual compliments of the morning, the colonel began to apologize by expressing his regret that the general should have had so much occasion to find fault at the careless manner of the duty having been performed, and turning towards me, said:

"You may go away."

I returned to the general's quarters and heard no more, of the matter; the two soldiers who had been confined were relieved before night, in consequence of some skirmishing taking place in the course of the day, and in which we had three men killed and a few wounded.

It was generally the case in the regiment, at that time, to send all the prisoners to their respective companies in the morning when the battalion was about to march off; and if the crime was not of a serious nature, the officer commanding the company was sometimes pleased to forgive, without recommitting the defaulter at night when we halted, and at which time our guard mounted.

At this time the clothing of the army at large, but the Highland brigade in particular, was in a very tattered state. The clothing of the 91st regiment had been two years in wear; the men were thus under the necessity of repairing their old garments in the best manner they could: some had the elbows of the coats mended with grey cloth, others had the one half of the sleeve of a different colour from the body; and their trousers were in equally as bad a condition as their coats.

The 42nd, which was the only corps in the brigade that wore the *kilt,* was beginning to lose it by degrees; men falling sick and left in the rear frequently got the *kilt* made into trousers, and on joining the regiment again no plaid could be furnished to supply the loss; thus a great want of uniformity prevailed; but this was of minor importance when compared to the want of shoes. As our march continued daily, no time was to be found to repair them, until completely worn out; this left a number to march with bare feet, or, as we termed it, *to pad the hoof.* These men being occasionally permitted to straggle out of the ranks to select the soft part of the roads or fields adjoining, others who had not the same reason to offer for this indulgence followed the example, until each regiment marched regardless of keeping in rank, and sometimes mixed with other corps in front and rear. To put a stop to this irregularity, the men without shoes were formed by themselves, and marched, under the command of officers and non-commissioned officers, in rear of the brigade.

It is impossible to describe the painful state that some of those shoeless men were in, crippling along the way, their feet cut or torn by sharp stones or brambles.

To remedy the want of shoes, the raw hides of the newly-slaughtered bullocks were given to cut up, on purpose to form a sort of *buskins* for the barefooted soldiers. This served as a substitute for shoes, and enabled the wearers to march in the ranks of their respective companies.

Our knapsacks were also by this time beginning to display, from their torn ends, their worthless contents; and as our line of march was in an opposite direction from our expected supplies, our exterior appearance was daily getting worse; but the real spirit of the soldier was improving, and I make little doubt but we would have followed our leaders to the extremity of Europe without grumbling.

We were getting hardier and stronger every day in person; the more we suffered, the more confidence we felt in our strength; all in health, and no sickness. The man in patched clothes and a piece of un-tanned hide about his feet, when he looked around him, saw others in some respects as ill appointed as himself; and he almost felt a pride in despising any new comer, with dangling plumes, plaited or crimped frills, white gloves, and handsome shoes—all good-for-nothing frippery to the hardy toil-worn soldier, the man of flint, powder, and steel, as he thought himself. His was the gloveless hand and the shoeless foot, that braved alike the cold and the heat, the toil of the field and the fatigue of the march; nothing came wrong to him; he started in the morning from his hard pillow and harder bed, required no time to blacken his shoes, but braced up his knapsack, regardless of the state of the roads or weather, and was ready to march off.

I have already mentioned that there was some skirmishing with the enemy this day, as we advanced. Extensive plantations of young trees lined the road, and in these the light troops of the enemy were posted to check our advance, and our light company was sent out to scour to the right of the road. Here we had three men killed and several wounded.

One of those who were killed had been doing the duty of pioneer, previous to this day; doubtless he had considered this a degrading duty, and had pressingly requested to be permitted to join the ranks; his request was granted; this was his first entry on the field since he obtained that indulgence, and here he fell. He lay on the field adjoining the road; someone had rifled his knapsack, but had thrown the blanket over him.

Having the general's baggage in charge, I was following the brigade with the guard and the mules, when I observed some soldiers examining to what regiment the killed belonged; one bore off the knapsack, but left the blanket carelessly cast on the corpse; a batman was making a prize of the blanket, and a Portuguese muleteer was about to take off the *kilt*. I could be at no loss to know to what regiment he belonged, as the 42nd was the only corps in the division that had that dress, and I desired one of the guard to recover the blanket and to spread it over the body, for we had no time to inter it; he sprung on the spoilers in an instant, snatched the blanket from the batman, and seizing the muleteer rather roughly, tumbled him into the ditch that lined the road; then spreading the blanket over the corpse, left it; but doubtless to be soon stripped again. Thus falls the poor soldier.

We continued to advance day after day, encamping by night, until the 4th of March, when, in consequence of the continued state of unfavourable weather, we were ordered into cantonments, and our brigade was quartered in the neighbourhood of Barcelon, nearly opposite to Ayre. We remained here until the 15th, when we crossed the river at Ayre, and encamped about two miles to the westward of that town. Here the regiment was joined by a draught from the second battalion, as well as by a considerable number of men from hospitals in the rear. The latter had, by some casual negligence of the officer in command, been surprised on their way to join by an inconsiderable party of the enemy's foragers; they had, however, been soon afterwards abandoned as a troublesome charge, and found their way to the regiment with this draught.

The day on which we received this augmentation was the anniversary of St. Patrick, a day well known in the British army by the indulgence taken in the deep carouse; and so far was it kept up in this camp, that if giving a loose to intemperance be a certain passport to the saint's favour, it was purchased to a certainty that day by at least three divisions of the army forming that encampment, which was, in consequence, designated by some "the drunken camp."

We advanced on the 18th, passed through Pau as the sun was setting, and encamped on the beautiful meadows east of that town.

Our movements were now directed towards Toulouse, but so protractedly, that it was the 5th April before we effected the passage of the Garonne, about three leagues below that city, and established ourselves on the right bank.

A few of the peasantry brought bread in small quantities to the camp, and met, if not with a profitable, at least with a ready market. But I have no hesitation in stating, that on the whole they were no gainers, in consequence of the pressure of the demand, and the haste of the buyers to slip off without paying.

One poor man had brought a few dollars worth, sold it in a few minutes, but had received little more than one dollar, so quickly had the purchasers made off after being supplied. He happened to recognise one of his cruel customers, and demanded payment, but the soldier insisted that he had given the dollar which the man held in his hand, and that he was waiting for the change; to the truth of which assertion he swore with the most determined audacity. No one, however, who knew Scully, believed him; but as no proof could be brought to the contrary, the poor man had actually to lose the balance, which, very likely, was falsely claimed. Lieutenants Farquharson and Watson, having as far as possible taken the dealer's part, made up a small sum for him, which perhaps left him no loser.

We broke up camp a little after midnight, on the morning of Easter Sunday, the 10th of April, and marched towards Toulouse. The moon shone bright in the unclouded heavens, and reflected a stream of light from the muskets of our advanced columns, for our arms had not then received the brown varnish that now "dims their shine." All nature seemed to enjoy repose, save our moving columns on every side, and the bullfrogs that gave to the midnight breeze their loud inharmonious croaking as we silently marched along.

The sun arose over the hills that stretch along the eastern banks of the Ers, and shone on forty thousand bayonets that glistened round the heights of Toulouse, where Marshal Soult stood, determined to oppose our advance.

General Pack's brigade was formed in contiguous columns of regiments to the left of the road leading to Toulouse. At this time the Spaniards, who were in advance and ascending the heights, were attacked with such fury that they gave way in all directions. It was apprehended that the enemy would have borne down upon us in the impetuosity of the movement, and we deployed into lines. The 79th regiment was at this time in front of the 42nd, and General Pack, anticipating a charge from the enemy's victorious and elated infantry, after thus scattering the Spaniards, gave orders to the 79th to receive them with a volley, immediately form four deep, face about, and pass through the ranks of the 42nd. The latter received orders to form four deep, as soon as the former had given its fire; let the line pass through, then form up, give a volley, and charge.

This was providing against what might have taken place, but did not, for the enemy was recalled, and the Spaniards were afterwards rallied.

We now moved off to our left, along a green embankment, a small lake or large pond on our left, and a wet ditch and marshy meadow on the right. The shot and shell were flying over our heads into the lake, but the range was too elevated to hurt us, and we ran along the bank until we came to a place where we could leap the ditch and form on the swampy ground beyond it. We had scarcely formed, when a strong column of the enemy, with drums beating a march, descended the hill in our front, and thinking from the nature of the ground that we should be neither able to advance or retreat, rushed down confident of success. For us to retire would have been scarcely practicable; the bank from which we had leaped down and over the ditch was too high in several places for us to leap back, from such uncertain footing; for we were sinking to the ankles, and sometimes deeper at every step; to advance was the only alternative, and it was taken.

The light companies of the division were by this time in our front, and without any hesitation dashed forward; we followed fast, and the opposing column re-ascended the hill and left us the undisputed masters of the valley.

We now ascended at double quick time, and the whole of the division crowned the eastern summit of the heights. Here we were exposed to a destructive fire of round shot, shell, grape, and musketry, while we had not as yet got up one gun, owing to the numerous obstructions that lay in the way. The ground we occupied sloped towards one of the main roads that runs over the hill to the city, and the fields on the opposite side of the road were in possession of the enemy, and extremely broken and intersected by deep cross-roads, breastworks, and redoubts; but could, from our present position, have been commanded by artillery, had it been practicable to bring a few guns forward; but this required some time, and indefatigable labour.

The light companies of the division advanced beyond the road, and maintained a very unequal skirmish with the enemy, who lay securely posted behind their breastworks and batteries, and in their redoubts, from all of which they took the most deadly aim. The 61st regiment was ordered forward to support the skirmishers, and became the marked object of the enemy's batteries, from which incessant showers of grape cut down that corps by sections, while Soult was perhaps not losing a man, being so safely sheltered from our musketry; it was therefore seen necessary to withdraw the skeleton of that regiment to the road, on which we had taken post after its advance; it was now warmly welcomed back, for its retreat was no defeat, and its loss was scarcely equalled by any corps in the field. Not a subaltern left the field without a wound, and the honour of the colours was assigned to sergeants.

The enemy, emboldened by this momentary success on his

part, began to advance towards the road, and our regiment was ordered to advance by wings and storm one of the redoubts.

Our colonel was a brave man, but there are moments when a well-timed manoeuvre is of more advantage than courage. The regiment stood on the road with its front exactly to the enemy, and if the left wing had been ordered forward, it could have sprung up the bank in line and dashed forward on the enemy at once. Instead of this, the colonel faced the right wing to its right, countermarched in rear of the left, and when the leading rank cleared the left flank it was made to file up the bank, and as soon as it made its appearance the shot, shell, and musketry poured in with deadly destruction; and in this exposed position we had to make a second counter march, on purpose to bring our front to the enemy.

These movements consumed much time, and by this unnecessary exposure exasperated the men to madness. The word *"Forward—double quick.'"* dispelled the gloom, and forward we drove, in the face of apparent destruction. The field had been lately rough ploughed or under fallow, and when a man fell he tripped the one behind, thus the ranks were opening as we approached the point whence all this hostile vengeance proceeded; but the rush forward had received an impulse from desperation, the spring of the men's patience had been strained until ready to snap, and when left to the freedom of its own extension, ceased not to act until the point to which it was directed was attained. In a minute every obstacle was surmounted; the enemy fled as we leaped over the trenches and mounds like a pack of noisy hounds in pursuit, frightening them more by our wild hurrahs than actually hurting them by ball or bayonet.

The redoubt, thus obtained, consisted of an old country farm-cottage, the lower part of its walls stone, the upper part mud or clay. It stood in the corner of what had been a garden, having one door to a road or broad lane and another to the garden; the whole forming a square which had been lately fortified on three sides by a deep but dry trench, from which the earth had been cast inwards, and formed a considerable bank, sloping inwards, but presenting a perpendicular face of layers of green turf outwards. The cottage served as a temporary magazine, and the mound or embankment as a cover to the enemy from the fire of our troops; and from this place our men had been dreadfully cut down.

It cannot be for an instant supposed that all this could have been effected without very much deranging our ranks, and as the enemy had still a powerful force, and other works commanding this, time would not permit of particularity, and a brisk independent fire was kept up with more noise than good effect by our small groups upon our not yet defeated enemy.

Our muskets were getting useless by the frequent discharges, and several of the men were having recourse to the French pieces that lay scattered about, but they had been as freely used as our own, and were equally unserviceable. Our number of effective hands was also decreasing, and that of the again approaching foe irresistible. Two officers (Captain Campbell and Lieutenant Young) and about sixty of inferior rank were all that now remained without a wound of the right wing of the regiment that entered the field in the morning. The flag was hanging in tatters, and stained with the blood of those who had fallen over it. The standard, cut in two, had been successively placed in the hands of three officers, who fell as we advanced; it was now borne by a sergeant, while the few remaining soldiers who rallied around it, defiled with mire, sweat, smoke, and blood, stood ready to oppose with the bayonet the advancing column, the front files of which were pouring in destructive showers of musketry among our confused ranks.

To have disputed the post with such overwhelming numbers, would have been hazarding the loss of our colours, and could serve no general interest to our army, as we stood between the front of our advancing support and the enemy; we were therefore ordered to retire. The greater number passed through the cottage, now filled with wounded and dying, and leaped from the door that was over the road into the trench of the redoubt, among the killed and wounded.

We were now between two fires of musketry, the enemy to our left and rear, the 79th and left wing of our own regiment in our front. Fortunately the intermediate space did not exceed a hundred paces, and our safe retreat depended upon the speed with which we could perform it. We rushed along like a crowd of boys pursuing the bounding ball to its distant limit, and in an instant plunged into a trench that had been cut across the road: the balls were whistling amongst us and over us; while those in front were struggling to get out, those behind were holding them fast for assistance, and we became firmly wedged together, until a horse without a rider came plunging down on the heads and bayonets of those in his way; they on whom he fell were drowned or smothered, and the gap thus made gave way for the rest to get out.

The right wing of the regiment, thus broken down and in disorder, was rallied by Captain Campbell (afterwards Brevet Lieutenant-Colonel) and the adjutant (Lieutenant Young) on a narrow road, the steep banks of which served as a cover from the showers of grape that swept over our heads.

In this contest, besides our colonel, who was wounded as he gave the word of command, "Forward," the regiment lost, in killed and wounded, twenty officers, one sergeant-major, and four hundred and thirty-six of inferior rank.

Meantime the Portuguese brigade was ordered to take possession of the evacuated redoubt, which was accomplished with little loss, for the enemy had been backward of entering, lest we might have been drawing them into an ambush, or had an intention of blowing up the cottage in which a considerable quantity of loose cartridges had been left near a large fire, by themselves when they were driven out, and most likely intended for that purpose against us, but we had removed the whole to a place of less danger.

Thus far the left flank of our army was secured; the Spaniards, further to the right, were making good their advances, our artillery was about getting posted on commanding eminences, while only one battery remained on the western summit in the enemy's possession, and before sunset it was stormed also, and all the heights overlooking Toulouse remained in our possession.

CHAPTER 10

The March to Bordeaux

It has been remarked by M. F. De Bourrienne, that "the French troops, commanded by Soult, made Wellington pay dearly at Toulouse for his entrance into the south of France." This remark tends to exalt the merit of Soult, as a commander, above Wellington, and the bravery of the French above the British. But, not to call in question the merits of either of the commanders, or of their respective armies, certainly, on this occasion, there was no great cause to boast of having made Wellington pay dearly for his victory.

Every nation has an epoch in its annals which raises its military or naval fame above others, during the same period; and this consideration may serve to prove, that courage, bravery, or enterprise is not a national inheritance of any people, but is the work of some master-spirit which draws it into action and leads it on.

The soldiers of France unquestionably proved themselves worthy of their great master, consequently deserve a soldier's praise. But with regard to Soult, it is but justice to the French to say, that the defence of Toulouse was no masterpiece of generalship. His troops certainly maintained the contest, worthy of the school in which they had been taught, and in a manner which the' conqueror of half the continent would not have blushed to witness.

When they retreated, it seemed to be by command; therefore, to retire when ordered was the duty of the soldier: but in a military point of view, the commander was to blame for ordering a retreat when the sacrifice of a few lives, in pushing forward, might have insured success. Had Wellington had the command of the French in the same position, and been supported by his own generals, double the number of troops, let them have been the best in the world, would not have reached the summit of those heights or wrested a single breastwork out of his hands. All the approaches seemed to have been rendered impassable for our troops, while great skill had been exerted in constructing batteries to bear upon those places which were supposed likely to cause us a momentary halt or a derangement in our ranks.

I may also remark, that there was a most unpardonable neglect in Soult permitting two divisions of our army to remain unmolested after they had crossed the Garonne on the 6th, as we were completely cut off for two days from the rest of the army, in consequence of the pontoon bridge having been thrown aside by a swell of the river, or, as some say, by a floating mill having been loosened from its fastenings and let down against the bridge.

I have already remarked that night, after battle, is always glorious to the undisputed victors, and whatever the loss may have been, the idea of it seems to be banished from our thoughtless minds. Here, however, by the first early dawning of the morning, let us more seriously cast our eye over this scene of slaughter, where the blood of the commander and the commanded mix indiscriminately together over the field.

Here lies many a gallant soldier, whose name or fame will never pass to another generation; yet the annals of our country will do justice to the general merit of the whole; from my feeble pen no lasting fame can be expected; time blots it out as I write; and even were I to attempt to pass an eulogy, it might be considered contemptible, from so humble an individual, by those who survive and witnessed the action; therefore, I shall leave to an abler pen to do them justice.

I trust I shall not be considered egotistical in saying that I had some narrow escapes this day; but what soldier entered the field, and came safe out of it, had not narrow escapes? A musket-ball struck my halberd in line with my cheek, another passed between my arm and my side and lodged in my knapsack, another struck the handle of my sword, and a fourth passed through my bonnet and knocked it off my head; had the ball been two inches lower, or I that much higher, the reader would have been saved the trouble of perusing this narrative.

The company in which I was doing duty lost four officers, three sergeants, and forty-seven rank and file, in killed and wounded. The officers were—Lieutenant D. M'Kenzie severely wounded, Lieutenants Farquharson, and Watson mortally wounded, and Ensign Latta killed.

I had occasion to remark, before entering France, of Lieutenant Farquharson having made me a present of a blanket, when my own was blown off my hut. He fell this day, by my side, on the road skirting the redoubt, and before we entered it. It was impossible to render him any assistance at the time, we were so closely engaged; but when the action closed, I returned and found him where he fell. He had been for a few minutes in the power of the enemy, and had been stripped of his sash, sword, epaulettes, and money, but no other violence had been offered to him. I got him conveyed to a house which was enclosed in another redoubt, and now filled in every place with our wounded. From this he was removed, on the morning of the 12th, to Toulouse, where he died of his wounds. In him, I may say, I lost a friend.

There was one officer of the regiment taken prisoner this day: he had lately joined us from the 1st Royals, in which he had been cadet, and had not the uniform of the regiment, but his deficiency of the uniform betrayed no lack of personal courage; the charm of the bonnet and plume, though wanting, did not make him less the soldier; he fell, wounded, near to Lieutenant Farquharson, at the side of the redoubt, as we entered it, and when we fell back he was made prisoner.

I have already mentioned, that before the regiment advanced to storm the redoubt, we were posted on the main road that passes over the heights. During the short time we were in that position, we had orders not to raise our heads above the bank, nor let the enemy see where we were posted; notwithstanding this prohibition, our sergeant-major, as brave a man as ever entered a field, was dispatched from the right flank to warn those on the left to comply with this order, for several were rising up occasionally and sending a bullet at the enemy, and thus perhaps defeating the intention of the order. He went; but though cautioned to stoop as he proceeded, he considered this unmanly, and never did he walk with a more upright dauntless carriage of the body or a firmer step: it was his last march; a bullet pierced his brain and stretched him lifeless, without a sigh.

There was a man of the name of Wighton in the regiment, a grumbling, discontented, disaffected sort of a character. He was one of the men attached to the tent placed under my charge on joining the regiment. Some men take all for the best; not so with Wighton, he took everything for the worst; indeed, his very countenance indicated something malignant, misanthropical, and even *sottish* in his disposition. He was a low, thick, squat fellow, with a dark yellowish swarthy complexion, and his broad face bore a strong resemblance to that of a Calmuc Tartar. As he rushed along the field, his front-rank man exclaimed:

"God Almighty preserve us, this is dreadful!"

"You be d—d," Wighton replied, "you have been importuning God Almighty this half-dozen of years, and it would be no wonder although He were to knock you down at last for troubling him so often; as for myself, I do not believe there is one; if there were, He would never have brought us here?"

The last word hung unfinished on his tongue; the messenger of death sealed his lips in everlasting silence*.

And here, thou troublesome, intermeddling, little man, the companion of my outward-bound voyage, thou who were reduced for thy ill-timed officiousness and insubordinate behaviour, here thou liest; death has for ever closed the scenes of this world over thee, and all thy faults and irregularities will soon be forgotten, and the remembrance of thee be no more in the regiment. Yet thy death, and the manner in which thou now liest, surrounded by the fallen companions of those whom thine own actions made thine enemies, afford me something for deep reflection. Thy ill-timed boasting and unjustifiable conduct reduced thee to carry the musket, yet a few short months cancelled thy faults, and the halberd and sword were again restored to thy unworthy hands; yet, strange to say, they were scarcely firm in thy possession, till, in company with those generous men whom thy turbulence made thine enemies, thou losest all that had been restored, and life also.

Yonder I see a young gallant hero stretched on the battlefield. Gallant Purves! thou hast sought fame far from the halls of thy fathers, and thou art now laid on the battlefield of a foreign land. But why that heavy sigh, my Mary? Why does a tear steal down your cheek as I bring the name of the youth to your remembrance? Is it because the days of childhood pass like a dream before your eyes, and that you see him, who now

---

* Since writing these sketches, I have had the pleasure of reading *"The Reminiscences of a Campaign in the Pyrenees and South of France,"* by J. Malcolm, Esq., late of the 42nd. It is contained in the twenty-seventh volume of Constable's Miscellany. Mr. Malcolm takes notice of Wighton by the name of Winnan, in page 288, and remarks that "He was considered the wit of the company, and a most profane one he was. After a long march in wet weather, before the tents had arrived, I have seen him sit down," says Mr. Malcolm, "in the rain, and sport with his misery by holding out his cold wet hands and praying for a little hell-fire to warm them." Perhaps Mr. Malcolm thought that Wighton was considered a wit; but I had a better opportunity of knowing him than Mr. M. had: Wighton was known as a dull misanthrope and general sceptic. Mr. Malcolm was the officer formerly alluded to having been taken prisoner.

lies low, a childish boy, stealing in amidst the cheerful circle of your playful companions at his father's gate, and then gliding off like a shadow? Why cherish those recollections? He is now laid low on his gory bed, and there shall the hardy thistle raise its *spiry* head to mark a Caledonian's grave. Around that spot many a brave man of the Cameron Highlanders breathed his last, in cheering on himself and companions to the fiery front of battle.

I might mention many acts of personal prowess, no less honourable to the brave men who performed than they were creditable to the corps to which those men belonged; but as relations of this kind are so often exaggerated, that they are and ought to be received with caution and even with a little doubt from the military journalist, particularly when he gives all the praise to his own corps, I shall therefore be sparing in giving them a place. Yet to pass over the whole would be unjustifiable in one who witnessed them, and considers that the bringing of the action itself into view may be the means of exciting others to emulate those acts of bravery which in the performance may be attended with greater success, and be better rewarded; while it wakes the memory of those who survived that day, and witnessed its interesting struggles, to the recollection of the incidents which I shall briefly state.

The contest that raged upwards of an hour around the redoubt, of which we had gained possession, was maintained without much regard to order or strict discipline; in short, it was rather tumultuous. Every man was sensible of the necessity of having order restored, but thought himself the only orderly man of all the rest, and his voice was heard over that of his commander calling out *"Form up"* In the mean time, his own attention was more engaged in keeping in the crowd, to load his piece, and afterwards pushing forward, to send a bullet to the enemy as often as he possibly could load and discharge, than attending to formation.

A grenadier of the 79th regiment, for both regiments (the 42nd and 79th) were somewhat intermixed, rushed forward, discharged his piece with effect, and suddenly turning the musket, so as to grasp the muzzle, dealt deadly blows around him; he fell, grasping one of the enemy in one hand and the broken firelock in the other. Another sprung up on the top of the bank, called on his comrades to follow, and with a loud cheer, in which many joined that did not follow, he rushed forward in the same manner as his brave companion had done, and like him shared a similar fate.

It is only in this disorganized kind of conflict that individual courage may best act and best be seen. In united orderly movements, the whole acquires the praise; and in this each individual is comprised, and proud of contributing his part to the honour of his corps, does his duty without attempting those feats of romantic daring which ancient historians record, but which modern tactics render nugatory or almost useless. Individual daring is lost in orderly movements.

Here fell Cunningham, a corporal in the grenadier company, a man much esteemed in the regiment; he was a married man, but young, and was interred before his wife entered the dear-bought field; but she had heard of his fate, and flew, in spite of every opposition, to the field; she looked around among the yet unburied soldiers to find her own, but she found him not. She flew to the place where the wreck of the regiment lay on the field.

"Tell me," she asked, "where Cunningham is laid, that I may see him and lay him in the grave with my own hand!"

A tear rose in the soldier's eye as he pointed towards the place, and twenty men started up to accompany her to the spot, for they respected the man and esteemed the woman. They lifted the corpse; the wounds were in his breast; she washed them, and pressing his cold lips to hers, wept over him, wrapped the body in a blanket, and the soldiers consigned it to the grave: mournful she stood over the spot where her husband was laid, the earth was again closed over him, and she now stood a lonely unprotected being, far from her country or the home of her childhood.

I should not perhaps say unprotected, for however callous our feelings may occasionally be, amidst a thousand distressing objects that surround us, any one of which, if individually presented to our consideration at any other time or place than the battle-field, would excite our sympathy, yet amidst all these neither the widow nor the orphan is left un-regarded, or in some measure un-provided for. In this instance, the officer who commanded the company to which Cunningham belonged having been severely wounded, sent for the widow; she became his sick-nurse, and under his protection was restored in decent respectability to her home.

Worthy generous M'Laren, thou art now no more; the wounds of that day preyed upon thy frame, shortened thy brief career, and bereaved the regiment of one of its best subalterns. Thou were always the soldier's friend, as well as the widow's protector. Shade of the brave, forgive this poor apostrophe to thy memory! It is the only offering a soldier can present; he plants it as a flower upon the green turf that covers thy cold remains; may it take root, and its blossoms excite some abler florist to grace the spot with greater beauty.

The only protection a poor soldier can offer to a woman suddenly bereft of her husband, far from her kinsfolk, and without a residence or home, would, under more favourable circumstances, be considered as an insult, and perhaps under these, from the pressure of grief that actually weighs her down, be extremely indelicate.

I make free to offer this remark, in justification of many a good woman, who in a few months, perhaps weeks, after her sudden bereavement, becomes the wife of a second husband; and although slightingly spoken of by some of little feeling, in and out of the army, yet this is perhaps the only alternative to save a lone innocent woman's reputation; and the soldier who offers himself may be as little inclined to the connexion through any selfish motive, as the woman may be from any desire of his love, but the peculiar situation in which she is placed renders it necessary, without consulting false feelings, or regarding the idle remarks that may be made, to feel grateful for a protector, and in a soldier, the most binding is the surest.

The sun gladdens again the face of the heavens, and throws his welcome rays over the field where the wreck of two armies lies un-interred. Thus we fall, cutting off and being cut off, the slayers but not the enemies of our race: look you to that, ye rulers of the earth!—we come but to obey.

Here lie the turbulent and the obedient, the oppressor and the oppressed, and who can tell whither their spirits have fled! Do they soar in friendship, sink in hatred, separate for ever with their scorn and hatred? or is every remembrance annihilated with the outpouring of their blood? Ah! ye reasoning sceptics, rob us not of the future hope; it is our sheet-anchor, and your own best safeguard.

That bright orb which now begins to warm our dew-moistened cheeks, moved on as unclouded in his career of yesterday as he promises to move to-day, regardless of the conflicting scenes of busy man, who falls without one mournful mark on nature's face for his untimely fall. Though the strife of armies raged over those heights, and the blood of thousands was poured out, yet all above moved on in summer brightness, and apparently saw without regard a mighty empire cease to exist, in the person who had raised it to command half the world.

Two nights we crowned the heights of Toulouse with our columns, and on the morning of the 12th we advanced after the retreating foe, who had left the city in possession of Wellington.

On the 15th the accounts of peace were made known to the army, and were received with every demonstration of joy. We now retraced our way, marched through Toulouse, so lately the scene of carnage, and took up our quarters about a league beyond it, at a large farmhouse and extensive wine-store in which we had been quartered on the 3rd and 4th of the same month, before crossing the Garonne; and as no movement was expected during that day, I obtained leave to return to Toulouse, in order to purchase some articles for the company to which I was attached.

Having settled my affairs as speedily as possible at Toulouse, I made all haste to return to the regiment, but to my astonishment, on approaching the place which I had left echoing with the busy hum of a hundred voices, I found all hushed in solitary silence. I proceeded up the avenue, where the embers of the expiring fires smoked against the walls; not a soldier was to be seen at the house or in the field; at last, as I approached the door, I saw my wife in tears, sitting on my knapsack. My appearance dispelled her grief, her heart leaped with joy, and, springing up, she embraced me.

We had now to find out the place to which the regiment had proceeded; and after pursuing the supposed route till after sunset, without any certain information whether right or wrong, we came to a small village occupied by the 74th regiment, and from the men of that corps met with a very kindly reception, and made welcome to quarters during the night. Early next morning, as we were about to proceed in search of our own regiment, the sound of the bagpipe struck our ears, and in a few minutes its welcome notes directed us to the regiment.

We proceeded by short stages, some nights in camp and some in quarters, until we reached Auch, a considerable town, beautifully situated on the face of a hill, overlooking the windings of the Gers. Vineyards, orchards, groves of olives and poplars, with hill and dale, diversify the face of this delightful country, and add greatly to the cheerful appearance of the comfortable farms and neat cottages which are thickly sprinkled over the rich uplands and surrounding valleys.

Our attention was more taken up here with balls and carousals than with field exercise. I should gladly pass over those scenes of intemperance, were it not that a few remarks may be useful, in as much as they serve to record that they were not altogether approved of, even by those who were led to join in them. And, I must further add, although not in justification of our intemperance, that our thriftless improvidence was our own loss, and doubtless we afforded a sufficient subject for ridicule; but the only harm done was to ourselves, while the vintners of Auch gained considerably by our folly.

Here our sergeants held their annual ball; this was a usage which had crept into the regiment after the battle of Alexandria in Egypt, perhaps at an earlier period, and if not laudable, was at least excusable, to keep in remembrance the actions of our old companions. The celebration of that event became sanctioned by custom. After the battle of Corunna, Egypt became only a secondary consideration, yet both days were admitted into the calendar of the regiment.

The storming of some outposts at Burgos, in Spain, was also admitted. Time and circumstances, this year, bad prevented the celebration of the anniversaries of those actions being noticed at their usual time: we were now enjoying ease, and like the troops of Hannibal at Capua, we were inclined to indulge ourselves as far as opportunity served and our inclinations led.

Our corporals followed the example set by the sergeants, the musicians that by the corporals, the drummers that of the musicians, and last, though not least, the officers' servants had a ball. Meantime the privates were not behind in paying their respects to the pleasures of the cup, for brandy was sold at the doors, and in the passages of our barracks, by strolling vendors, for one penny a gill, and a quart of good wine was to be had at the wine-houses for threepence.

These proceedings were put a stop to at last, and it was high time. What could appear more ridiculous than seeing sergeants, who, in all regiments, are or may be considered the select of the ranks for intelligence, temperance, and orderly behaviour, marching to their barracks about sunrise, preceded by a band of music attempting to play. This debasing exhibition concluded by our drawing up on the mall in front of the barrack, to show ourselves sober to the rest of the regiment, by dancing a reel, to convince them we were so. It was something to the credit of the women, that they had retired before this public trial of sobriety or drunkenness took place.

We are all unanimous, when we meet to resolve on how we are to act, in decrying this manner of commemorating the anniversary of a past achievement; but we want firmness to stand to our resolutions when we meet for enjoyment: the voice of the gay confounds that of the grave; and when cheerfulness is the order of the day, no one has so much of the saint as to oppose the sinner. Therefore, I hesitate not to say, that the celebration of those anniversaries is a growing evil, the means of keeping up a system of dram-drinking and drunkenness, and should be put a stop to.

We had only lain in Auch about five weeks, when we were ordered to proceed to Bordeaux for embarkation. After resting one night at Valence and another at Condom, we came to Narac, a considerable town, pleasantly situated on the Baise, a small river, by means of which a navigable communication is open to the Garonne, thence to all the ports on that river, and its canals, from the Mediterranean to the Atlantic. Narac seems to possess a considerable trade; and although the buildings are inferior to those of Condom, the general appearance of comfort, cleanliness, and active industry of the inhabitants is in its favour, while the trade of Condom seems to be on the decline.

Our regimental stores, consisting chiefly of spare clothing which had been received before we left Auch, were put on board a vessel here, on purpose to lessen our land conveyance, and placed under my charge to Bordeaux. The other regiments of the division that accompanied us on the line of march adopted the same plan, and appointed suitable escorts. Thus, while the division continued its route for Bordeaux by land, the baggage and escorts, under the command of Lieutenant Ford of the 79th, dropped down the Baise, the banks of which during the greater part of its course limited our view, until we were wafted in upon the mighty current of the Garonne.

Here a new scene opened all at once to our view. The country to our right had lain hid behind the trees and copses along the margin of the Baise, while the abrupt ascent of the left bank threw its shadow over the stream, and hid the setting sun from our view as we approached the conflux with the master stream, which seemed to chide its tributary's lazy approach, and to suck our bark on to its more ample bosom. The beautiful country on the right bank of the Garonne now presented its gaily diversified vest, rich with vineyards, orchards, groves of olives, and fields of rising grain, while the princely mansions and comfortable looking cottages reflected from a thousand windows the golden gleams of sun and sky.

Our sudden debouchement upon the river, from between wood and willow-shaded banks, enhanced the beauty of the landscape at the conflux of the Baise; for the country further down, on either side of the river to Bordeaux, was either hid from our view by the banks, or presented no interesting scenery worth remarking; neither hill nor forest, pending rock or castellated tower, throws its shadow over the course of our solitary bark; no town or village, with its busy port, to attract our attention or excite a wish to tread the drowsy shore.

Two vessels were all the craft we met during the two days that our bark continued to speed her way downwards; and by the exertions required in working against the stream, we were led to conclude that the trade carried on by this channel was neither extensive nor profitable. About twenty men were employed in hauling one of the vessels forward, and about twelve were engaged with the other; for steam had not then been brought into use to give its powerful assistance to the mariner. But what tended not a little to impede their progress upwards, was the swollen state of the river, in consequence of recent rains, and perhaps the snow had not yet been entirely dissolved on the Pyrenees, from which it takes its rise.

Soon after sunset, we put into a small cove on the right

bank, where we lit a fire, cooked some meat, enjoyed a comfortable refreshment, and reposed in peace over our charge until morning, when we again held on our course.

Past noon we again put into a creek on the left bank, where we were detained a few hours in consequence of some business which the master of the vessel had to transact in the neighbourhood. This circumstance afforded us time to light a fire and prepare some dinner.

The sky, which had been heretofore cloudless, and the day excessively hot, began to appear gloomy; the master was inclined to remain there until next day, but all the passengers were anxious to proceed, and yielding to their solicitations, he set off with the falling tide.

As evening approached, the clouds rose thicker on the horizon, and emitted vivid flashes of lightning. We were now within a league of Bordeaux, darkness closing fast around us, and the stream bearing us rapidly along. The lightning became more vivid as we proceeded, and the thunder, which had been growling at a distance for some time, burst in astounding peals over our heads.

We now approached the shipping on the river, with a receding tide; but so closely were we enveloped in darkness, that no object was visible around us, save that which the flashes of lightning suddenly opened to our view; and the helmsman, either struck by the electric fluid or by terror, let go the tiller; the peal of thunder and rash of rain that instantly succeeded this occurrence excited considerable alarm on board, when, to add to our danger, our neglected helm no more guiding our vessel in safety down the stream, she bounded against the cable of a ship at anchor, reeled round, upsetting those who were standing, and a general shriek of distress burst spontaneously from the female passengers on board: fortunately we cleared the fore part of the ship and ran under her chains, to which our people clung so effectually, that they succeeded, with the able assistance of the ship's crew, in securing our charge alongside, where it remained until morning.

Bordeaux presents a line of buildings, fronting the Garonne, somewhat similar to that which Prince's Street of Edinburgh presents to the valley called the North Loch; and though not so uniform in height and architecture, is no less attractive to the eye of a stranger, by its diversified appearance. But notwithstanding that Bordeaux from the river bears a strong resemblance to the new town of Edinburgh from the North Loch, or, more properly speaking, from Prince's Street Gardens, yet the objects on either side of the river are dull and insignificant when compared with our Modern Athens.

No romantic height, such as Arthur's Seat or Salisbury Crags, rises in its neighbourhood; no proud elevation, such as the Calton Hill, crowned with monuments and lined with splendid edifices, shoots from its bosom; no grey rock, with its castellated battlements, like that on which Edinburgh Castle stands, looks down with frowning dignity on its busy streets; no piles of buildings, many stories high, similar to those of James's Court, the Bank of Scotland, the Exchange, and many others, look over the river to Bordeaux, as these do, in our northern metropolis, over the North Loch to Prince's Street.

In short, all the beauties which Bordeaux can boast, and they are not few, rest on the same extensive plain with itself, and consist of its hospitals, markets, fountains, parks, and walks, and, above all, its majestic river.

We disembarked near the ruins of an old fortification, close to the quay, and found within its walls what we then considered comfortable quarters. Comfortable only in comparison with what we had been accustomed to since we left England; for even here we had neither bed, nor furniture, nor kitchen utensils, but the lodgings were good and dry. Meantime the regiment performed its march by land, and encamped at Blanchford, about six miles below the city.

Bordeaux at this time exhibited a scene of great mercantile bustle; the opening of the port to British shipping and colonial produce, which had for a number of years been interdicted, invited an immense number of traders, while the demands of the army gave a stimulus to the agriculturist, the merchant, and the mechanic; in short, every class had occasion to rejoice at the change which had taken place by the restoration of the Bourbons.

The Frenchman is not so intolerant a bigot as the Spaniard. The latter seldom passes a chapel, an altar, or a cross (and they are without number in Spain), without uncovering his head and making the sign of the cross on his face, mouth, and breast; covering himself with this imaginary antidote to evil, he walks on full of his spiritual invulnerability. The Frenchman, on the other hand, though professing the same religion, walks on as regardless as a Scotch Presbyterian. Whether this disregard to the church of Rome and its symbols of worship has been long existing in France, or only crept in during the revolutionary era, I know not; however, since the restoration of the Bourbon dynasty, the clergy are zealously bent on bringing about a superficial display of religion.

At the time we arrived at Bordeaux, the clergy were assembling for some public occasion, and this afforded us an opportunity of witnessing one of those splendid pageants which in all countries exclusively professing the Catholic faith are held in the greatest respect, and looked upon with as much reverence as if the members which compose them were the delegates of heaven.

On the day appointed, the procession proceeded from one of the churches. A dignitary of the clergy walked beneath a splendidly embroidered canopy, supported by four bearers; before him was an altar resting on two sedan poles; in his hands the Host or consecrated wafer was held, and occasionally elevated; more than a hundred priests in superb vestments walked in procession. On each side of the altar were boys swinging, by silver chains, small silver censers with burning incense, while a number of children bedecked with gilded artificial wings, so as to represent cherubs, walked under the guidance of the religious in the procession.

The streets, through which this imposing pageant passed,

displayed a thousand devices from balconies, windows, doors, and house-tops. Altars were erected in different places, splendidly ornamented, each with its own patron saint dressed in very costly robes. An immense number of strangers, as well as the greater part of the inhabitants of the city, crowded to witness the spectacle; all uncovered as the Host passed, and not a few fell on their knees, while showers of rose-leaves, from ten thousand hands, dropped on the uncovered multitude below.

The regiment lay encamped at Blanchford until the 21st of June, when it embarked for Ireland. On the 29th we cleared the mouth of the Garonne, spread all our canvas to the breeze, and soon lost sight of that land, where we had left the bones of our bravest behind.

CHAPTER 11

To Ireland—then Abroad Again

We had been three days at sea, with delightful weather, all hearty and cheerful. The morning meal was in preparation, the decks were washed, our berths all cleaned, and the bedding airing in the freshening breeze. Some were employed fishing with hook and line, others washing, some mending, and not a few smoking tobacco.

One of our sergeants, named Warnock, apparently in health, asked from one of the smokers a *whiff* of his pipe; it was given; but before the smoke passed twice from his mouth, he fell down a lifeless corpse. Medical aid was at hand, but Death had made sure of his mark, and the body was consigned to the ocean next day.

Warnock had been on the sick-list and absent from the regiment during the two last campaigns, and had joined us after the spilling of blood was over. Soldiers seldom admit that real sickness is the cause of one's absence, and hesitate not to impute the absence to a desire of avoiding hard duty and field danger. Thus the absentee is considered a scheming dissembler, and called a *sconce,* until death proves him no liar: then the common saying is, "Poor fellow, after all, he has been ailing."

Our voyage, though somewhat protracted by calms, was very pleasant; and we arrived at Cork, in good health and high spirits, in the month of July. After being quartered in Cork barracks two weeks, we marched to Naas; thence, after another two weeks' halt, we were ordered to Kilkenny.

We paraded for the march by daybreak on the morning of the 17th August, and the effects of the night's orgies still played on the senses of those who had been led to indulge too freely in the parting cup with our countrymen of the Forfar Militia, then stationed at Naas. Among the number of the slightly inebriated was our assistant sergeant-major, an active, clever, obedient man when sober; but one of the most domineering, headstrong, irascible, insubordinate, provoking fellows, when drunk, that was in the regiment; in consequence of which he had been repeatedly reduced to the ranks, but his supposed qualifications as a drill brought him still forward. Having neglected to make arrangements in his detail for a rearguard, he ordered me to turn out for that duty.

It is not a justifiable point to remonstrate respecting turns of duty, but by the intemperate manner in which I was commanded, I was led to question the propriety of being thus made the selected one, passing several others before me in the *roster;* and the usual apology of a soldier for shunning a troublesome duty passed my lips, by saying:

"It is not my turn."

"How do you come to know that it is not your turn?" he exclaimed: "Who appointed you the regulator of the duty? You had better take the command, Mr. Independence, as you are above complying with the orders of your superiors." Thus he went on in a tirade of insulting and irritating abuse, without even permitting an interval for reply, as if intentionally, for the purpose of exciting to resistance, so as to constitute a crime; but I had been too long in the military school to commit myself by allowing my passion to operate against myself.

Yet there are limits to patience, and perhaps I might have been forced beyond them, had not the timely call of the adjutant drawn off the insulter to answer regarding the disposal of some defaulters; and by the time he returned, he was less obstreperous, and I more yielding; for there is no advantage in the army by persisting in advocating right from wrong, when your opponent has it in his power to make the first unfavourable report, and to poison the ear of the superior who is to decide.

Indeed, no duty is more disagreeable than that of the rear-guard on the first day's march of a route; acquaintances banging on the men, causing them to quit their ranks, loiter behind, and get drunk, for which the non-commissioned officer in charge of the guard gets the blame.

Our route was by Athay and Carlow to Kilkenny, where we arrived on the 19th August, and were quartered in it and its vicinity upwards of eight months. Here an order was issued for the payment of all arrears due to the regiment. This appeared to be a most Herculean task to our pay-sergeants; for they had always a most decided aversion to paying money. The cause of this aversion was, that a most detestable practice had crept into the regiment (I may say into the army), of allowing the pay-sergeants to serve out shirts, shoes, and other necessaries, as the men required them: no matter though a man was a pound or two in debt, this made him the more certain customer of his sergeant. Shirts were charged at the rate of eight shillings, and a pair of shoes the same price; these articles were privately sold afterwards by the men at the rate of five shillings, sometimes less, and they found their way back to the sergeant again.

By this means a shirt or a pair of shoes frequently passed twice or thrice through the sergeant's hands in one day. It was therefore no wonder that he was backward in paying money, when he had so much interest in withholding it. This led to a system among the men of selling their necessaries when it suited their convenience, and ultimately to drunkenness, crime, and punishment: for woe to the poor fellow who had the misfortune to sell out articles which had not originally come through the hands of his pay-sergeant; the full weight of the law fell on his shoulders.

It may seem something extraordinary that this sort of dealing passed on without detection, or how the men did not complain of this sort of mercenary work to the officers in charge of companies. But this forbearance may be ascribed to the general disposition of the men: they had been accustomed to this manner of dealing, they were satisfied with the system, and grumbling constituted no part of their general character; besides, those who were most prone to this traffic were in debt, or at least considered so, when the full amount of their continental arrears was not to their credit, *viz.* six months' pay to each rank, after deducting sixpence per day for rations.

The time was now come when this was to be paid; and the general commanding in Kilkenny allowed us three days free of all public duty, in order to have all accounts settled and drink-devoted money expended.

I here received upwards of twenty pounds sterling of arrears due to me; and if the officer commanding the company had not personally attended at the payment, it might have been the object of twenty instalments.

I had applied for money to my pay-sergeant on our arrival at Cork, and met with evasions far from satisfactory. I complained to my officer, and from him to the colonel; for instead of six months' arrears being due to me, there were more than ten months due. I had received nothing but rations, chargeable off my pay, from the day I left Portsmouth until we entered Cork. I had asked my pay-sergeant for money before leaving France, but met with an evasive answer. He had the effrontery to say, that when an order was given in June to pay off the arrears due on the preceding 24th January, that no man was considered in credit, at that period, unless he had six months' arrears due at the back date which the order mentioned. That implied as much as to say, "You had only five months' arrears due to you on the 24th January last, therefore you were one month's in debt at that period."

By such an opinion as this, I would have required to let my pay run on a twelvemonth before I would be in credit; I could not allow such reasoning to be just, and now, when I had occasion for money, I demanded it. The colonel promised me redress, called for the pay-sergeant, who exonerated himself by stating that an order had been issued for completing the men with necessaries, and were he to pay the sum to which I was entitled, he could not comply with that order. The colonel promised to see further into the matter, and there it rested, for I made no more complaints.

The case appeared so decidedly clear to me, that refusing to pay the amount due after deducting the six months' arrears, to be left for a future payment, was nothing less than encouraging a system of truckling, which ought to have been repressed. What had one soldier's credit to do in covering another's debt, or why his pay have been withheld without his consent, evidently for the purpose of enabling a pay-sergeant to purchase shirts, shoes, &c. for men already in debt, and that he might have the benefit of turning the arrears to his own account, in the event of the creditor's sudden death?

In laying open this system of corruption, in the interior economy of the regiment, I am far from offering an exaggerated statement, as I am certain it will meet with a ready corroboration from every soldier who was then in the regiment; and although I thus limit my observation, I might add, the system was not confined to one regiment, it was pretty general in the army.

I shall state one instance that came under my observation, when the regiment was quartered in Auch. A regimental order was issued about the 30th April, desiring the arrears due to the men on the preceding 24th October to be paid off: this left the arrears of the six following months, namely, from November to April inclusive, still to their credit. The pay-sergeants had complied with this order, with the exception of two or three, who found some excuse for protracting the payment of individuals. I happened to be in the room of one of those cashiers when one of the men not settled with entered and civilly asked the sum to which he was entitled; this was refused: he then begged to have five shillings, until such time as it would be convenient to let him have the balance. This was also refused; the man was naturally led to offer reasons for pressing the request; but the other repulsively ordered him off, and shut the door contemptuously at his heels as he retired. The soldier, when thus turned off, went immediately to the officer commanding his company, and from him met with a more kindly reception; he sent him back to get the sum demanded. I had not left the sergeant's room, when the man re-entered and reported the result of his application; but this was of no consequence, he was as peremptorily ordered off as he had been before; and as he left the apartment in sullen silence, the sergeant exultingly exclaimed:

"I'll be d—d but he shall call me sir and gentleman, before he gets a single *chovy**.*"

This manner of repulsing a soldier, when civilly and respectfully asking that to which he had a right, was unusual, and could not fail to excite vindictive feelings; and I am certain there was not another sergeant in the regiment who would have acted in such a manner. To do the pay-sergeants justice, although they wanted to make the best of the money that they could, they were not repulsive. But this one was an exception: he was the adjutant's clerk, of whom I have already bad occasion to take notice, and perhaps may again, in the course of this narrative.

From witnessing this, and other neglected applications for money, I forbore soliciting any from the time I joined the battalion until my arrival at Cork, where I made the application just mentioned. Our weekly pay, however, was regularly issued after this, conformably to the regulations for home service. Such were the good old times, when complaints were seldom made, and when made, not regarded.

The three days' indulgence, granted by General Gordon, opened a bright prospect for the publicans of Kilkenny. The 36th regiment and the Somerset Militia performed the gar-

---

* A small Portuguese coin, about the size of a farthing.

rison duties. Our barrack-guard was the only duty imposed upon us; and I, equally as unfortunate on this occasion as on leaving Naas, was pitched upon for the first day's duty, notwithstanding that there were eight before me on the *roster*. Like many more grumbling *wights*, I remonstrated, but to no effect; some were pay-sergeants, and the sobriety of some others was questionable. These were sufficient reasons, and somewhat satisfactory, so far as concerned myself; for perhaps there are few soldiers but have a little pride in being regarded by their superiors as capable of discharging a difficult or troublesome duty.

I was granted a supernumerary, or an assistant, on purpose to aid me in repressing drunken broils, and so far as possible keep the guard sober; his name was Robert May, a good sort of a careless tippling old soldier who had been lately appointed sergeant. I thus had the name of an assistant, but in fact got none of his assistance. The men who mounted guard, however, were considered the least intemperate of the regiment; yet there are times when the most rigidly abstemious will lose sight of themselves by suffering the overflowing cup of intentional kindness to approach their lips, and yielding to the pressing invitations of cheerful companions, participate in the prevailing conviviality; and I regret that some of my guard so far lost sight of their duty as to get themselves insensibly inebriated. I shall offer no excuse for having confined them as prisoners.

He who is entrusted with a duty, if he fail to perform it, must stand to the consequences; and he who is entrusted with a command which he cannot enforce, is undeserving of it: their place was supplied by others. Five times successively the guardroom and its adjoining dark closet were filled with noisy turbulent prisoners, and as often ejected and sent to their barracks, released through the kind interposition of the adjutant, in consequence of the crowded state of the guard-house.

It is a well known duty in the army, that every officer and non-commissioned officer in the command of a guard, is enjoined to visit the sentries frequently by day and by night, and in his report he must state having done so. In compliance with this regulation, I went to visit the sentries posted in rear of the barrack after sunset. This was a considerable round at that time. I left May to answer for the guard until I should return. I had no sooner departed, however, than he withdrew to one of the neighbouring ale-houses. Meanwhile the visiting officers for the day (Captain M'Intosh and Lieutenant Nicholson) made their call, and there was no sergeant to answer for the guard. The sergeant-major was called and ordered to place me under arrest; luckily he could find no one to replace me. As for May, there was no more notice taken of his absence than although he had had no occasion to be present.

The captain lodged in a house which I had to pass in returning to my guard; I saw him and the subaltern enter it, but little did I surmise that I had occasion to report to them what I was about; the sergeant-major, however, having got notice where I was, met me, told me what had passed, and permitted me to call on the captain on purpose to exculpate myself. My excuse was fully admitted, and I was dismissed with a caution not to leave my guard in charge of another until relieved.

I certainly had reason to feel thankful to the sergeant-major for permitting me to exonerate myself before my arrest was reported to the commanding-officer; for he could have been justified in denying access to the captain.

I think it is proper to suggest to those who have the arrangements of public or regimental duties, to make every non-commissioned officer take whatever duty may present itself, in his proper turn, unless he be recently appointed and the duty apparently difficult. All cases where exemptions are made in consequence of intemperance, imbecility, or the like, should be considered as an imposition on the service. Why indulge men given to intemperance by exemptions? Why permit imbeciles to hold the very lowest situation of command over a soldier in the army? If such characters have by chance crept or leaped into place, by cringing sycophancy, mean, dangling servility, or otherwise, let them be hazarded with the duty which they have considered themselves qualified to perform; if they fail, their places can be filled up, and the service sustain no loss by the degradation of those who are incapable of performing it, or who incite others to trespass instead of preventing them.

The three days passed over, and the regiment resumed its public duties in the garrison. I may remark, that our intemperate assistant sergeant-major, who acted rather uncivilly towards me on leaving Naas, was very deservedly reduced to the ranks at this time.

We were joined in this place by the second battalion of the regiment, which was incorporated with ours, and we now formed one battalion. Among the men who joined were a considerable number who had been taken prisoners of war by the enemy on the different retrograde movements of the army in the Peninsula, all of whom laid claim to their pay during the time they had been in durance, as well as for compensation for loss of knapsacks and necessaries, all of which claims were sustained, and afterwards paid.

It may not be improper to question how far claims of this kind ought to be admitted. Men who have been wounded and left on the field, or in hospital, and abandoned to the mercy of the enemy; men who have been placed in charge of posts in rear of the army, for the purpose of checking the enemy's advance, defend their posts until forced to yield to overwhelming numbers, deserve the best regard of their country, and cannot be too well rewarded; they deserve more than their pay, for they have been cut off from the common enjoyments of a soldier's freedom, limited though it be; from every expectation of rising in the service; and all this to enable their more fortunate companions to have the satisfaction of enjoying those appreciated chances. But certainly those who fall into the hands of the enemy through their own negligence, stubbornness, or intemperance, ought to feel deeply the effect of their past misservice, and of their country's displeasure afterwards, for having served it so un-faithfully.

A considerable number of detachments are furnished from the garrison of Kilkenny to the different villages and hamlets throughout the surrounding district, and the regiment having been upwards of four months without being called upon to take any of these detached duties, was now ordered to relieve the different parties of the 83rd regiment, which composed part of the garrison.

I was sent in command of a small party to Tulleroan, an inconsiderable group of mud cabins and low thatched houses, about six miles from Kilkenny. The unfavourable report we had received regarding the disaffected turbulent disposition of the inhabitants, caused us to receive their congratulations on our arrival with repulsive sulkiness; they were poor, and we considered them intrusive when they approached the door of our little smoky dark hole of a barrack; and all their generous offers of disinterested service were indignantly refused.

I really cannot look back upon that part of my conduct with any degree of satisfaction; yet I was only acting up to received instructions. Had I and my party continued to conduct ourselves in the same repulsive manner in which we had commenced with our neighbours, we might have had just occasion, on leaving the place, to give a different ac-count of their behaviour towards us than we now do. Indeed, they could have been submitted to very little inconvenience or trouble by our indifference or contempt, but we must have felt theirs considerably, as *every* article of provisions had to be procured through their agency, otherwise the party must have been weakened and the men harassed by sending three or four off, every second or third day, to Kilkenny to make purchases; and in this there was no small chance of hazarding the sobriety of the men to irresistible temptations among those who were doing duty in that town. Our kind neighbours, however, prevented, in a great degree, the necessity of sending to a distance for our supplies.

Two constables were attached to our party, relieving each other alternately, once every two weeks, so that one only remained at the barrack: from both we received an exaggerated account of the state of the public feeling around us. One, in particular, was always sounding the tocsin of alarm in our ears. A party of *Whiteboys, Shanavites, Caraviecs,* or *Carders**, had been seen in such a direction, several shots had been heard in another, yet no one came forward as the seer or the hearer; all was verbal report, through a long transmission from one credulous person to another, until it reached the constable, and a report had to be forwarded to the magistrate; in consequence of which a party was ordered out towards the reported place of alarm, on purpose to ascertain the certainty or cause; and after patrolling the country for miles, disturbing the peaceable and causing alarm, it returned satisfied that the report was founded in falsehood, and that no cause existed to suspect that the people had been otherwise employed than in their usual domestic or agricultural pursuits.

I must here remark, that there is rather a false idea abroad respecting "Irish barbarism," as it is called. In no two countries of the world do the manners and customs of the rural population resemble each other more closely, perhaps, than that of the Highlands of Scotland and that of Ireland.

There is not a man from the north or west Highlands, and who had been a resident there forty or fifty years ago, but will acknowledge that nothing was more rare than to hear of a country fair having passed over without bloodshed or broken bones. I perfectly recollect hearing, when I was a boy, the people asking at those who were returning from the fairs of Keith, Glass, Auchindore, Sliach, &c:

---

* Names assumed by certain parties associated for obtaining local reforms, chiefly agrarian.

141

"Well, wis thir ony feghts at the market the day?" (or yesterday). If the reply was in the affirmative, the questioner rubbed his hands, scratched his shoulder or elbow, itching with delight, saying, "Ha! that's a sign o' gude times, we'll get cheap meal this year."

But if the reply was in the negative, then no joy was expressed; on the contrary, there was some remark about hard times, or "Gude auld times," adding, "Fouk's gettin' o'er wise now-o'-days, God help us, the auld spirit's broken down," and such like observations.

And the questioner, in his fretfulness at being deprived of the news of a fight, would exclaim, "Fare wis the Goulds fan ther wis nae feghtin' at Glass?" or " Fare wis the Barclays fan ther wis nae feghtin' at Sliach?" and such like questions.

This is still the case in Ireland, at least among the rural population; there are certain family names, noted for club-law, in the neighbourhood. But there is this difference: in Scotland we had no peace-preservers to raise a "hue and cry" of murder when there was no lives lost; cuts and bumps were thought nothing of, and gave no alarm; but in Ireland it is the very reverse; the numerous tribe of attorneys are looking out for work: blood is murder, knocking down or tripping over is killing; and the report appears next day, in some neighbouring newspaper, headed "Barbarous Murder, Shocking Outrage, Dreadful Barbarity, &c. &c," detailing the cause and consequence of the quarrel, appealing to the injured and insulted feelings of the nation in general. But remark, the reporter most likely is one of our peace-preservers, and the report closes by giving great praise to Mr. So-and-so, with his constabulary force, who succeeded in suppressing the riot at great personal risk, and in having lodged the principal aggressors in jail. Perhaps the article states further: "We regret to hear that one or two of the constable's fusils went off in the affray, whereby one or two men were slightly wounded."

Perhaps the constables have got their clothes torn, a fusil broken, or some personal bruise or contusion; all or any of which form pleas for criminal prosecutions, and burdening the country with oppressive local taxes, and not a life lost after all the clamour, save that of some outrageous vagabond, who thus deprives the gallows of its due and the lawyer of his fee.

Nothing is more certain, than that the country was in a perfectly peaceable state, with regard to constitutional allegiance. There were local associations of a secret nature, but they were more for controlling what the different parties considered local oppression than government authority; and every individual in our neighbourhood vied with each other in little acts of kindness and a willingness to be serviceable to the party.

Were we scarce of fuel, they would freely lend us until a supply could be obtained; if provisions were short, they would find some person to supply us; in fine, our ill-natured manner of receiving their welcome, when we first came among them, did not excite their ill-will towards us; they had been used to such ungenerous treatment. We were not a little annoyed, however, during the first four weeks of our lodgement, by a crowd of country-people congregating about our door, on Sundays and holidays, and even stepping in, some to warm themselves, and some to light their pipes, without any bad intention; but as every thing regarding them had been represented in the worst light, we should have been acting very unguardedly had we not been ready to meet danger, without manifesting a fear of it. But to prevent it was better; and by an easy representation of my wish to some of our neighbours, I found our barrack become less an object of public curiosity.

Among the readiest of those people to serve us was Ned Magrath, an honest, hardy, industrious brogue-maker. This man was ready to serve us on all emergencies; and we certainly had not a few wants. Placed as we then were, so remote from the market from which we drew our supplies, in the depth of winter, and having no contract for provisions with any person, our supplies were irregular, and sometimes very limited, waiting for chance conveyances.

After we had lain a few weeks in this place, a heavy fall of snow covered the face of the country to a considerable depth, in drifted wreaths, which closed up the roads and prevented us getting fuel. Magrath, after making every inquiry in the neighbourhood to procure us some, but without effect, had recourse to an expedient which, though not uncommon in that place, was new to us. Having procured for us about two bushels of coal-dust, or *culm*, he went to a place where clay was to be had, cleared off the snow, and dug up a quantity sufficient to mix with the *culm*; this we brought to the barrack, and after pounding the two together until thoroughly mixed, made up into balls the size of six-pound shot: these, when dried, made a strong durable fire.

This supply, however, failed; the snow continued longer than usual to obstruct the roads, and the people, not accustomed to lay up a store for the winter, were in want themselves, and under the necessity of gathering the withered sprigs along the sides of hedges and plantations. In this emergency we were again supplied by our indefatigable neighbour, but by means of which popular superstition forbade him taking advantage on his own account.

The limb of a large hawthorn-tree, designated the *monument,* had been cast down by a storm, some years previous to our arrival, and although in its prostrate state a useless encumbrance on the field, yet popular superstition had rendered it so far sacred that neither man nor woman would presume to lop off one of its decayed branches. This was pointed out as offering itself to our hands; but as we had a verbal agreement with the poor landlord of the barrack to provide us with fuel, we had no desire to trespass on the local prejudices of the people in supplying ourselves, until his exertions to furnish us ceased to be effective; we were then under the necessity of doing something for ourselves; for he was so poor that the neighbours trusted more to our paying in money for what they lent us on his account than to his repaying in kind.

In the mean time, we made particular inquiry concerning this tree, and what entitled it to the name of *monument* and the regard shown towards it, lest we should by a premature seizure incur the ill-will of the inhabitants.

In the vicinity of Tulleroan are several thorn trees, designated *monuments;* each has some superstitious legend attached to its notoriety in the traditional tales of the Tulleroans. One of these monuments stands on the right side of the road, where it is crossed by the burn of Kilmanagh, and is famed for being a metamorphosed trooper, who was thus transformed by a rebel priest. The latter had been in concealment for some time, my informant says, "invisible," but he happened to be observed by this trooper, and was about being made prisoner, when by the power of the holy God, and the intercession of the ever blessed Virgin, the priest transformed the trooper into a tree.

He had no sooner wrought this miracle than he was surprised by another straggler of the same troop, and was about being made prisoner again, but the man of God convinced the captor that he must have been born and baptized within the pale of the holy Roman Catholic church, otherwise he could not have discovered his materiality, as he had been invisible to all the other troopers who had passed, with the exception of the one who now stood before him transformed into this dwarfish tree. The astonished trooper is said to have acknowledged the truth of what the priest said, suffered him to escape, and became a living witness to the transformation.

That which gave celebrity to the one devoted to warm our winter hearth, was possessed of no less interest, and may be depended upon as being as certain as the other. This tree stood in the middle of a small enclosure, opposite a farm-house, a few perches beyond the chapel, and once consisted of two limbs, forking from the trunk, some feet from the ground. I shall let pass the telling of the fabulous and conflicting accounts of the cause of its original claim to veneration, and mention a circumstance which is held as authentic by the oldest inhabitants of the place.

A remarkably severe snow-storm and close winter, perhaps worse than that which we were experiencing, had occasioned the scanty store of fuel in the neighbourhood to be consumed, and the fanner on whose ground the tree stood, not paying so much regard to its sanctity as to his family comforts, resolved to apply some of its exuberant branches to domestic use. The hatchet was raised to strike, when he descried one of the ricks in his *haggard* on fire: casting his hatchet aside, he ran towards the farm, but on passing the sacred circle of the tree, he perceived all as settled, as calm, as cold, as smokeless, and comfortless around his dwelling as when he left it.

Astonished at the strange deception, he returned on purpose to execute the work he had been about to commence. A second time the same wonderful appearance astonished him; the hatchet was still erect in his hands, and he saw the flames spreading from the *haggard* to his dwelling-house: throwing down the hatchet, he flew to save his family, but as he approached the phantasm disappeared, and all around assumed its cold and cheerless aspect.

Ashamed to return empty-handed to his cold hearth, he again resolved to benefit himself by a few branches, be the consequences what they would. It is not certain whether he directed his eye this time towards his premises or only to the bough of the tree, which he struck with the axe, but at the first blow a splinter of the wood struck out one of his eyes and obliged him to desist from his sacrilegious enterprise; and from that time the tree was regarded more sacredly than ever, until nearly a century had passed away, when one of the limbs was torn by a violent storm from the decaying trunk, cast to the ground, and lay a useless encumbrance, yet still possessed of so much importance from the above incident as to deter the inhabitants from meddling with it.

An object held sacred by any class of people ought to be approached with respect, even by a stranger, let his opinions be ever so different from those of its worshippers. He who smites a priest on the right cheek, may smite the left also and be forgiven; but to scoff at the idol which the priest adores, is the sin which will never be forgiven by the worshippers of that idol.

My party were a set of young fellows who felt it no degradation to make themselves as comfortable within doors sis possible, and, without doubt, they were more successful gleaners and nibblers along the hedge-sides than the poor infirm creatures, who were frequently thankful to us for permission to boil or roast a few potatoes at our fire; and we had no reason to doubt but our success in that particular inclined them to direct our attention to the object which Magrath had pointed out to us.

Thus, all willing to promote our comfort, we applied to the superintending magistrate, Mr. Barton, from whom we met with no direct refusal; and we soon cleared the ground of its useless cover, and supplied ourselves with a fortnight's fuel.

Indeed, I should not wonder although this achievement were by this time blended with the history of the remaining branch. Perhaps it will be said that the *genius* of the tree rested not until a victim fell to its wrath, and that one of the party afterwards returned and shot himself.

The place which we occupied as a barrack was perhaps as good as could be obtained; however, it was but a smoky, worthless, low mud-cabin, admitting the rain or melting snow through its ill-thatched roof, and the water through its insecure foundation. Before the door ran a small streamlet, the receptacle of all the dirty water from the different cabins, stalls, and sties of the whole hamlet on that side of the road; but of this we had no great cause to complain, as the rains and thaws, which were frequent during our sojourn, carried off all impurities, although occasionally overflowing to our worn down threshold.

Poor as Tulleroan was, we left it with regret: to the people at large we owe our best wishes, and that we carried with us a share of theirs we have no cause to doubt. And thou, the reverend coadjutor of the parish priest, were not remiss in encouraging that spirit of goodwill which sprung up after our arrival and continued increasing until we departed. From thy hands we received such books* as made the long winter nights pass pleasantly away; thy good sense made thee forbear to offer us volumes of divinity, thou gavest us therefore what some would have called "the not needful", but thou didst give us the truly acceptable, and I trust we are no further from the door of grace yet, than if thou hadst loaded our table with all the works of the holy fathers of thy church.

Permit me, in the name of all who survive of that party, to express our gratitude for thy kindness. And were my thanks worthy of acceptance, they ought not to be the last of being offered to thee, our reverend curate of Kilmanagh; often hast thou visited our little smoky barrack, called our attention to thy divine exhortations, kneeled down amongst us, and offered up thy prayers to heaven for our happiness. Ah! Mr. Cauldfield, we who kneeled around thee had much need of thy intercession to Heaven in our behalf: the religious tracts with which thou hast unsparingly furnished us are but seldom read, and we are all too much of the careless cast to be really sincere in our devotions; yet we know thy zeal for our spiritual welfare, and if thy ministry has been uselessly cast away upon some, we hope it has had a good effect upon others; and wherever the fortune of war leads us, we shall gratefully keep in remembrance thy kindly visits and well-intentioned instructions.

We left Tulleroan, on the 22d of April, for Kilkenny, from which we again marched, on the 27th, for Cork, to embark for the continent.

During the time we had been at Tulleroan, one of the party became acquainted with a young woman with whom he fell in love, and he fancied that she loved him. She was a serv-

---

* The priest had the kindness to lend us Goldsmith's Works, History. &c. The book-reading man was so seldom gratified with the loan of a book, that, when offered, it was considered a great compliment.

ant in a public-house, to which his visits, before leaving that place, had been too frequently made, and he was about being sent off from the party to headquarters, when the unexpected route called off the whole.

This unfortunate man had been for several years a prisoner of war, and whatever might have been his habits before he was taken prisoner, I cannot say, but he certainly returned a very dissipated character; and having received a considerable amount of back pay, or prison-money, as it was called, he was enabled to visit the ale-house as often as the barrack, and when the pot was before him, he was always in love with the filler of it.

Having left Tulleroan without declaring his love to the young woman, or at least without her acknowledging her regard for him, he left his company as it marched out of Kilkenny, went to Tulleroan without leave, and having been disappointed in his expected interview, shot himself in the vicinity of that place.

On our arrival at Cork, no time was lost in preparing for active service; all our old and apparently debilitated hands were invalided and left behind; four women to each company were permitted to accompany us, and the rest were sent to their respective homes or parishes.

We embarked at the Cove, 4th May, 1815, and proceeded with a fair wind for Ostend.

We were not so fortunate as we had been on former voyages with respect to the weather, for we had a very stormy passage until we passed Plymouth, the hatches being frequently fastened down to prevent the waves, which were washing over the decks, from filling the hold; and one of our transports had to take shelter in Milford Haven, where she lay about a week: it was our better fortune to dash through the billows until we reached Ostend.

CHAPTER 12

At Quatre Bras

Nothing could appear more astonishing to us, coming directly from the land of rocks and mountains, than when we disembarked on the dyke or bank which seems to keep back the ocean, and looked down on the far extended plain below, where neither rock nor mountain presented itself as a refuge for the inhabitants from the threatening billows that seem to rise above the land and beat against the apparently artificial barrier.

Peace had given us only a few months' repose in the arms of our country, when we were thus hastily and unexpectedly called hither to oppose the rebel forces of the great Napoleon, who, rushing from his exile at Elba to the eastern shores of his lately abdicated empire, struck the world with astonishment. France hailed him back with all its wild enthusiastic pride of military fame. His former companions in arms crowded to his standard, and from the Pyrenees to the Alps, from the Mediterranean to the Atlantic, all were in motion. He advanced in the pride of power, and seized without a struggle the throne and crown of a long dynasty of kings.

The sovereigns of Europe beheld with astonishment this man of boundless ambition, with whom no obligations were binding, no oaths sacred, and no promises regarded that interfered with his personal interest, and, rising up in their wrath, poured forth their armies like overwhelming streams to oppose his yet unconsolidated power.

Britain roused her soldiers from their peaceful slumbers, and sent them forth as the first of Europe's sons to prove their arms on the extensive plains of the Netherlands; and she sent, as their leader, as brave a general as ever drew a sword, and as fortunate as ever fought a battle; in him the troops put every trust, and in their bravery he placed implicit confidence.

I have already mentioned, that on leaving Ireland, four women had been permitted to follow each company of the regiment, and accommodation on board ship afforded them to Ostend. We had now disembarked, and boats lay on the canal ready to convey us into the interior of the country; but as we were stepping on board, an order was received, importing that only two women would be allowed to proceed with each company.

This was a great disappointment, and no small cause of grief to those who had to return without any preparation for such an unexpected separation, or any provision but that which the liberality of their country might allow, or the hand of charity present, to carry them to their distant home. Those who had gotten on board of the boats waiting for our conveyance were turned out, notwithstanding their sighs and tears, given in charge to a guard, and quartered in a barrack at Ostend. Meanwhile we moved slowly up the canal, and left the poor weeping women behind to form their future plans of proceeding, and make arrangements for following the fortunes of their husbands.

Our hearts not being of the softest kind, soon lost the momentary impression of grief that had been made by the late affecting scene, and we approached Bruges as cheerful as if nothing of the kind had occurred, with the exception of the few sorrowing husbands whose wives had been detained.

The country, from Ostend to Bruges, is one extensive plain; from Bruges to Ghent a few undulations may be seen. The banks of the canal are lined with stately trees, which afford an agreeable shade to the passenger, and give a charming effect to the otherwise unvaried course on which we were proceeding.

Ghent bursts on our view as we emerge from the dark grove of elms and approach the crowded quay. We disembark, enter the city, receive billets on the most respectable inhabitants, and meet with a cordial reception.

Several days elapsed before the rest of the regiment arrived; storms and contrary winds had forced them into Milford Haven, as I have already mentioned, and reports had given them up for lost; but better fortune favoured them, and they arrived all safe, and were quartered in this wealthy, hospitable city. Indeed, no words can do justice to the kindly manner in which we were treated.

We were invited to sit at the same table with our landlord; coffee was offered to us early in the morning; breakfast, dinner, and even a supper, was prepared for us with no less attention than if we had been kinsmen visiting the family. In short, had we continued a few months in this place, we might have forgotten that we were soldiers, and the inhabitants must have considered us burdensome.

We had been only two days in Ghent, when the women left at Ostend found their way to the regiment; they were again conveyed back to the same place from which they escaped, and there closely watched; yet in a week or two they eluded the vigilance of the sentries and joined their husbands once more, and as no official reports were made to their prejudice, they followed the fortunes of their husbands during the campaign, along with those who boasted the privilege.

It may not be improper to remark, that on all occasions of troops being despatched to the scene of expected hostilities, women should not be permitted to accompany them. If an exception is made in one single instance, it only gives room for pressing and almost irresistible applications from others, and throws the performance of a very painful duty, namely, refusing permission, on the officers commanding companies. Every private soldier conceives that he has as good a right to this indulgence for his wife as the first non-commissioned officer in the regiment, and certainly he is right; she will prove much more useful than one who, instead of being service-able, considers herself entitled to be served, assumes the conse-quence of a lady without any of the good qualifications or accomplishments of one, and helps to embitter the domestic enjoyments of others by exciting petty jealousies that other-wise would never exist.

It is generally the case, in selecting women to follow the army to a foreign station, that choice is made of those without children, as they are considered more capable of performing the services that may be required of them than those encum-bered with a family; this, though just as regards our wants, is not so with respect to many a well-deserving woman, who is thus cast on the public or left to her own exertions, which too often fail her in the endeavour to support herself and children, while the childless woman is selected to profit from that circumstance.

I am no great theorist, but I am certain that much might be done to obviate the necessity of soldiers' wives being bur-densome to the public, by adopting proper means for their support*. Why should not the soldier contribute part of his pay towards the maintenance of his family at home? In fact, it ought to be stipulated that he should do so, before permission be given him to marry. If no women were permitted to ac-company the army (I mean on a hostile campaign, for I see no

---

* A woman who is permitted to accompany her husband receives a half ra-tion free; a child above seven years, one-third; and one under seven years, a quarter of a ration; and although this is but a very trifling allowance, would it not be much batter to give it to those of good character who are not permit-ted to accompany their husbands? I must also remark, that on foreign stations, where this allowance is made to the women and children, it will be found that the least necessitous are the first to apply, and the first to be placed on this benevolent list. I have seen privates' wives, with three or more children, without rations; while the wives and children of sergeant-majors and quar-termaster-sergeants were getting them. If the extra rations for women and children be a colonial, charge, it might be added to the charge for those who have been kept at home, and given to them, and none given to those who are permitted to accompany their husbands.

objection that can be made to the women being permitted to follow their husbands in times of peace, wherever their regiments may be stationed), the married men might earn more than their daily pay, by washing for the officers and non-commissioned officers, and to any of the single men who are not inclined to wash their own linen, and thus be enabled to make the larger remittances.

The fixing of a residence also, for his young family, ought to be held out as a stimulus for this arrangement. How few soldiers' children have any interest in the word *home,* notwithstanding its welcome sound to the ear of the cottage-born boy, to whom it brings to mind all the pleasant recollections so firmly impressed on his mind that age is incapable of effacing them. It may be said by some that this view of home is too limited, and that a soldier ought to have no fixed spot in his country to call his own; but this is bad reasoning; for the man who prides himself in that spot where he intends to make a settlement, will pride himself also in acquiring and preserving a character that may give him a title to respect amidst the circle in which he means to pass the evening of his life; while the man of the mob, or the man of the world, is too often as careless of his country as he is of his character, and when unable to serve his king and country any longer, will be found shifting from place to place and satisfied with none.

We left Ghent on the 27th May, and after resting one night at Alost, proceeded to Brussels, where we were as well received as we had been in the former city.

A circumstance occurred, during the time we lay in Brussels, which a feeling of respect for the parties concerned might make me forbear to record; but as it is by pointing out how crimes originate that we are enabled to avoid falling into the like afterwards, and as it is better to prevent crime than to have the merit of discovering it and bringing the offender to punishment, I shall give it a place in this memoir.

In Ghent all our great-coats were taken from us, and in place of them we received blankets; these, for quality and size, were such as an army had never received before, and such as were worthy of England to give. They were intended not only to be our covering in camp, but, upon any emergency, to serve for a tent also. We had them all looped and prepared for this purpose: it is needless for me to explain the manner in which this was done; we all knew perfectly well that they were for that purpose, and each man had a particular interest that his comrade should not destroy or make away with this useful article.

In Ghent, or in Brussels, each blanket could have been sold readily for nearly twenty shillings, a most tempting price for a soldier who saw many a fine article before his eye that he was anxious to possess, yet could not obtain, but by some unjustifiable means, such as the disposal of his own necessaries.

The sale of the blankets began with a few of the worst characters in the regiment: three men joined together and sold one; then taking shreds of the other two, made up the number by sewing the two shreds up the middle, thus preserving the appearance of complete ones, but diminished one-third in breadth. The money was divided or devoted to drink, and all kept quiet for several days; at last, however, the secret was divulged, and some of the very best characters, without any exception, suffered themselves to be drawn into the nefarious traffic which the worst had begun.

The circumstance having been reported to the colonel, the regiment paraded in a field for exercise without the walls of the city, and as on all occasions we paraded under arms with our knapsacks and appointments, just as if we had not been to return to our quarters, he had no difficulty in finding out the defaulters. Here every man was made to unpack for an inspection of necessaries. This was a time when an artist might have seen something in the human countenance and attitude worthy of his pencil, in delineating the stern, the sullen, the surprised look of many a poor luckless fellow as he threw his pack down before him.

The blankets were examined, the defaulters turned to the

rear, a drumhead court-martial assembled on the spot, the halberds fixed in the front, and as punishment was awarded, it was then and there inflicted.

The man who would attach blame to our colonel, for this prompt but severe decision, knows little of military affairs. He is now no more, and cares as little for what I can offer in justification of his actions as for what the guilty, who suffered punishment, may say to brand him with unforgiving severity. It must be allowed, that those men were placing, though not intentionally, his commission at stake; had he winked at their proceedings, he might have led a half-naked regiment out of Brussels; and instead of seeing us comfortably covered in our night's bivouac, beheld us shivering under useless shreds of blankets, and himself called to account by the general for the curtailment.

We were now anticipating some hard work, and every man was impatient to be at it.

On the night of the 15th June, we were roused from our peaceful slumbers by the sounding of bugles, the rolling of drums, and the loud notes of our Highland bagpipes, which threw their wild warlike strains on the midnight breeze, to awaken the plaided sons of Caledonia to arms.

Until daybreak of the 16th we stood to our arms on the streets of Brussels, and here we were served out with four days' provisions for each man. The grand ball was broken up, and our Highland dancers, who had been invited to display their active movements before the assembled lords, ladies, and military chieftains, were sent to their respective regiments, to prepare for other sport—that of glorious battle.

I have heard some passing animadversions upon our great commander, for thus passing away time upon the eve of so momentous an affair as that about to take place. I think, as a soldier, and one who was on the spot, I have as good a right to give my opinion concerning it as any of those croaking politicians who were hundreds of miles from the scene of operations; and in giving my opinion, I give it as that of every soldier who was in Brussels at the time, and I believe we are not the worst judges of what is most likely to forward a ready assembling, or a speedy concentration of the troops, in order to attain the end in view.

Nothing, then, I do not hesitate to affirm, could have tended more to promote our great commander's views than this ball. Most likely it was not intended or given purposely to accelerate those views, but fortunately it was the cause of promoting them, and of forwarding the cause of European independence and freedom in general.

Owing to this general assembly of all our principal officers, the duke had not only all his personal staff about him, but that of the generals under his command. They, again, had around them all the commanding officers of corps, to whom they could personally communicate their orders. The unusually late hour at which the dispatches from the scene of hostilities had arrived, and the information respecting the intended movements of our allies, in consequence of their having unexpectedly had to retreat from the bravely contested field, might have changed all our commander's plans.

If this should have been the case, he had all those about him to whom he could communicate his designs, without passing hours at the desk and sending orderlies off to the quarters of officers in a city, the language of whose inhabitants was foreign to us. All this trouble, happily for us and for Britain, was saved by this fortunate ball.

As we are now about to proceed to a field where the fate of France, perhaps of Europe, is to be decided, I trust I shall be permitted to confine my remarks to the narrow limits within which a soldier acting in the ranks of his regiment may be supposed to have acted. I shall thus, I hope, escape the risk of hazarding the trust-worthiness of my narrative, and avoid the imputation of presuming to enter upon matters having no direct relation personally to myself.

Leaving, therefore, the *general* operations of the field to the general historian, I shall confine my statement to the incidents which passed within the circle of my own observation; and in doing so, I shall indulge myself with less hyperbole than some may think the occasion would excuse, although perhaps with more than the good sense of a philosophic spectator, had there been such a one on the field, would tolerate.

On the morning of the 16th June, before the sun rose over the dark forest of Soignes, our brigade, consisting of the 1st, 44th, and 92nd regiments, stood in column, Sir Denis Pack at its head, waiting impatiently for the 42nd, the commanding-officer of which was chidden severely by Sir Denis for being so dilatory. We took our place in the column, and the whole marched off to the strains of martial music, and amidst the shouts of the surrounding multitude.

We passed through the ancient gate of the city, and hundreds left it in health and high spirits who before night were lifeless corpses on the field to which they were hastening.

As we entered the forest of Soignes, our stream of ranks following ranks, in successive sections, moved on in silent but speedy course, like some river confined between two equal banks.

The forest is of immense extent, and we continued to move on under its welcome shade until we came to a small hamlet, or *auberge*, embosomed in the wood to the right of the road. Here we turned to our left, halted, and were in the act of lighting fires, on purpose to set about cooking.

We were flattering ourselves that we were to rest there until next day; for whatever reports had reached the ears of our commanders, no alarm had yet rune on ours. Some were stretched under the shade to rest; others sat in groups draining the cup, and we always loved a large one, and it was now almost emptied of three days' allowance* of spirits, a greater quantity than was usually served out at once to us on a campaign; others were busily occupied in bringing water

* One English pint. There were four days' allowance of bread, and three days' of beef and spirits, issued, before leaving Brussels, for each man.

and preparing the camp-kettles, for we were of the opinion, as I have already said, that we were to halt there for the day. But, "Hark! A gun!" one exclaims; every ear is set to catch the sound, and every mouth seems half opened, as if to supersede the faithless ear that doubts of hearing.

Again another and another feebly floats through the forest. Every ear now catches the sound, and every man grasps his musket. No pensive looks are seen; our generals' weather-beaten, war-worn countenances are all well known to the old soldiers, and no throb of fear palpitates in a single breast; all are again ready in column, and again we tread the wood-lined road.

The distant report of the guns becomes more loud, and our march is urged on with greater speed. We pass through Waterloo, and leave behind the bright fields of Wellington's fame—our army's future glory and England's pride. Quatre Bras appears in view; the frightened peasantry come running breathless and panting along the way. We move off to the left of the road, behind a gently rising eminence; form column of companies, regardless of the growing crop, and ascend the rising ground: a beautiful plain appears in view, surrounded with belts of wood, and the main road from Brussels runs through it.

We now descended to the plain by an echelon movement towards our right, halted on the road (from which we had lately diverged to the left), formed in line, fronting a bank on the right side, whilst the other regiments took up their position to right and left, as directed by our general. A luxuriant crop of grain hid from our view the contending skirmishers beyond, and presented a considerable obstacle to our advance.

We were in the act of lying down by the side of the road, in our usual careless manner, as we were wont when enjoying a rest on the line of march, some throwing back their heads on their knapsacks, intending to take a sleep, when General Pack came galloping up, and chided the colonel for not having the bayonets fixed. This roused our attention, and the bayonets were instantly on the pieces.

There is something animating to a soldier in the clash of the fixing bayonet; more particularly so, when it is thought that the scabbard is not to receive it until it drinks the blood of its foe. Call me not blood-thirsty for expressing myself in this unfeeling manner; it is harsh, but it is just. I must not allow my own feelings to betray me into a display of those sympathies which I have not seen existing.

Our pieces were loaded, and perhaps never did a regiment in the field seem so short taken. We had the name of a *crack* corps, but certainly it was not then in that state of discipline which it could justly boast of a few years afterwards. Yet notwithstanding this disadvantage, none could be animated with a fitter feeling for the work before us than prevailed at that moment.

One half of us had never been on a campaign before; therefore, when an old soldier began to tell, and he was often telling, of what he had seen and suffered, he engrossed all the attention and talk, with the exception of a few remarks that puffed up his pride more and more to enlarge; and our young hands, thus kept in a less assuming position than that to which they laudably aspired, were anxious to be led to face the enemy. We had others burning with rage, resentment, and all the evil passions that mingle with our nature, and who could find no fit object around, on which they could pour out the vials of their wrath: still smarting under the effects of punishment for a crime which they could not allow themselves to think of great importance or disgraceful, and the less so as so many had participated in it. These were the men who had been recently convicted of making away with the blankets.

We were all ready and in line—*"Forward!"* was the word of command, and forward we hastened, though we saw no enemy in front.

The stalks of the rye, like the reeds that grow on the margin of some swamp, opposed our advance; the tops were up to our bonnets, and we strode and groped our way through as fast as we could. By the time we reached a field of clover on the other side, we were very much straggled; however, we united in line as fast as time and our speedy advance would permit.

The Belgic skirmishers retired through our ranks, and in an instant we were on their victorious pursuers. Our sudden appearance seemed to paralyze their advance. The singular appearance of our dress, combined no doubt with our sudden debut, tended to stagger their resolution: we were on them, our pieces were loaded, and our bayonets glittered, impatient to drink their blood. Those who had so proudly driven the Belgians before them, turned now to fly, whilst our loud cheers made the fields echo to our wild hurrahs.

France fled or fell before us, and we thought the field our own. We had not yet lost a man, for the victors seldom lose many, except in protracted hard-contested struggles: with one's face to the enemy, he may shun the deadly thrust or stroke; it is the retreating soldier that destruction pursues.

We drove on so fast that we almost appeared like a mob following the rout of some defeated faction. Marshal Ney, who commanded the enemy, observed our wild unguarded zeal, and ordered a regiment of lancers to bear down upon us. We saw their approach at a distance, as they issued from a wood, and took them for Brunswickers coming to cut up the flying infantry; and as cavalry on all occasions have the advantage of retreating foot, on a fair field, we were halted in order to let them take their way: they were approaching our right flank, from which our skirmishers were extended, and we were far from being in a formation fit to repel an attack, if intended, or to afford regular support to our friends if requiring our aid.

I think we stood with too much confidence, gazing towards them as if they had been our friends, anticipating the gallant charge they would make on the flying foe, and we were making no preparative movement to receive them as enemies, further than the reloading of the muskets, until a German orderly dragoon galloped up, exclaiming, *"Franchee! Franchee!"* and, wheeling about, galloped off.

We instantly formed a rallying square; no time for particularity; every man's piece was loaded, and our enemies approached at full charge; the feet of their horses seemed to tear up the ground. Our skirmishers having been impressed with the same opinion, that these were Brunswick cavalry, fell beneath their lances, and few escaped death or wounds: our brave colonel fell at this time, pierced through the chin until the point of the lance reached the brain. Captain (now major) Menzies fell, covered with wounds, and a momentary conflict took place over him; he was a powerful man, and, hand to hand, more than a match for six ordinary men. The grenadiers, whom he commanded, pressed round to save or avenge him, but fell beneath the enemy's lances.

Of all descriptions of cavalry, certainly the lancers seem the most formidable to infantry, as the lance can be projected with considerable precision, and with deadly effect, without bringing the horse to the point of the bayonet; and it was only by the rapid and well-directed fire of musketry that these formidable assailants were repulsed.

Colonel Dick assumed the command on the fall of Sir Robert Macara, and was severely wounded. Brevet-Major Davidson succeeded, and was mortally wounded; to him succeeded Brevet-Major Campbell (now Lieutenant-Colonel on the unattached list). Thus, in a few minutes, we had been placed under four different commanding-officers.

An attempt was now made to form us in line; for we stood mixed in one irregular mass—grenadier, light, and battalion companies—a noisy group; such is the inevitable consequence of a rapid succession of commanders. Our covering sergeants were called out on purpose that each company might form on the right of its sergeant; an excellent plan had it been adopted, but a cry arose that another charge of cavalry was approaching, and this plan was abandoned.

We now formed a line on the left of the grenadiers, while the cavalry that had been announced were cutting through the ranks of the 69th regiment. Meantime the other regiments, to our right and left, suffered no less than we; the superiority of the enemy in cavalry afforded him a decided advantage on the open plain, for our British cavalry and artillery had not yet reached the field.

We were at this time about two furlongs past the farm of Quatre Bras, as I suppose, and a line of French infantry was about the same distance from us in front, and we had commenced firing at that line, when we were ordered to form square to oppose cavalry. General Pack was at our head, and Major Campbell commanded the regiment. We formed square in an instant. In the centre were several wounded French soldiers witnessing our formation round them; they doubtless considered themselves devoted to certain death among us seeming barbarians, but they had no occasion to speak ill of us afterwards; for as they were already incapable of injuring us, we moved about them regardful of their wounds and suffering.

Our last file had got into square, and into its proper place, so far as unequal companies could form a square, when the *cuirassiers* dashed full on two of its faces: their heavy horses and steel armour seemed sufficient to bury us under them, had they been pushed forward on our bayonets.

A moment's pause ensued: it was the pause of death. General Pack was on the right angle of the front face of the square, and he lifted his hat towards the French officer, as he was wont to do when returning a salute. I suppose our assailants construed our forbearance as an indication of surrendering; a false idea: not a blow had been struck nor a musket levelled; but when the general raised his hat, it served as a signal, though not a preconcerted one, but entirely accidental; for we were doubtful whether our officer commanding was protracting the order, waiting for the general's command, as he was present.

Be this as it may, a most destructive fire was opened; riders, cased in heavy armour, fell tumbling from their horses; the horses reared, plunged, and fell on the dismounted riders; steel helmets and *cuirasses* rung against unsheathed sabres, as they fell to the ground; shrieks and groans of men, the neighing of horses, and the discharge of musketry, rent the air, as men and horses mixed together in one heap of indiscriminate slaughter. Those who were able to fly, fled towards a wood on our right, whence they had issued to the attack, and which seemed to afford an extensive cover to an immense reserve not yet brought into action.

Once more clear of these formidable and daring assailants, we formed line, examined our ammunition boxes, and found them getting empty. Our officer commanding pointed towards the pouches of our dead and dying comrades, and from them a sufficient supply was obtained.

We lay down behind the gentle rise of a trodden down field of grain, and enjoyed a few minutes' rest to our wearied limbs; but not in safety from the flying messengers of death, the whistling music of which was far from lulling us to sleep.

The general historian of the day may with justice remark how well the other regiments distinguished themselves in the field: my silence detracts nothing from their merit: praise from so humble a writer as I can give no celebrity to their achievements, which deserve to be recorded by one whose writings will descend to future ages; mine sinks to oblivion, and, with myself, will soon be forgotten. Say, then, should not this foreboding thought arrest the pen that would presume to trace achievements already on the records of history, and, in spite of the writer's foresight, waste itself in hopeless attempts to please?

Afternoon was now far spent, and we were resting in line, without having equalized the companies, for this would have been extremely dangerous in so exposed a position; for the field afforded no cover, and we were in advance of the other regiments. The enemy were at no great distance, and, I may add, firing very actively upon us.

We had wasted a deal of ammunition this day, and surely to very little effect, otherwise every one of our adversaries must have bled before this time. Our commanding-officer cautioned us against this useless expenditure, and we became a little more economical.

Our position being, as I have already observed, without any cover from the fire of the enemy, we were commanded to retire to the rear of the farm, where we took up our bivouac on the field for the night.

Having so far detailed that part of the action most particularly connected with the regiment to which I belong, without alluding to the general proceedings of the day, I shall make free to take notice of the French accounts as given by Giraud, as he may be considered less partial to the cause of Britain and its allies than an English historian. He commences by stating:

> The advance of our left wing commenced about two o'clock in the afternoon. The high standing corn, and the numerous copses and ravines which occurred between Frasne and Quatre Bras, prevented our troops from ascertaining either the number or real position of the English. No precaution had been taken to clear away the underwood, and thus facilitate the march and the deploying of the infantry, and the division of Foy, which formed the advanced guard, experienced much difficulty in advancing through the execrable roads. At length it arrived at Quatre Bras, and attacked the position with the bayonet; but it was received with a fire so incessant and murderous, that it was evident we were fallen into an ambuscade. Our troops, however, rushed with courage and impetuosity on an enemy whose force they disdained to calculate. The first brigade of the division of Bachelu, which led the right of the attack, imprudently advanced without waiting until the columns that should have supported it were formed,

and being suddenly charged by three Scotch regiments, which a wood on the right had concealed from our view, was driven back in disorder. These regiments paid dearly for their success, for, eagerly pursuing the fugitives, they unexpectedly found themselves exposed to the fire of the second brigade and part of the division of Foy, and were almost annihilated.

In the mean time our troops, being engaged in a difficult and unfavourable country, were unable to advance. The fire of the English was terrible, and it was necessary to have recourse to other dispositions.

Marshal Ney, who had hitherto thought the enemy less numerous than it actually appeared to be, now precipitately fell into the contrary error, and at four o'clock in the afternoon sent in haste for the first corps. It should be recollected that this corps was almost three leagues in the rear of the field of battle; that hitherto the marshal had not expected or was prepared for any serious affair; that, consequently, he had not considered this corps as his reserve; that its distance would not permit him to hope, at whatever time he might send for it, that it could arrive soon enough to co-operate in any decisive movement; and that its absence ought not to have influenced the dispositions which he was still enabled to make to re-establish a combat, in which we must acknowledge that it is impossible to recognise the precaution and foresight of an old and experienced general.

Between five and six o'clock in the evening the dispositions for a new attack were completed, and our columns advanced to drive the enemy to the left upon Nivelles.

Had this manoeuvre succeeded, it would have effected a complete separation between the English and the Prussians. The attack was made with partial success. The enemy soon gave way, but it was only to gain a wood on the left of the road, which he had lined with infantry, and where he formed himself into squares to receive us. The cavalry of Count Kellerman displayed the most brilliant courage, but without any result worthy its efforts. The marshal then caused the 8th and 11th cuirassiers to advance. Had this charge been made home it would have been decisive, but it only procured a cuirassier of the 8th the opportunity of seizing one of the enemy's standards. These two regiments, having passed through the fire of the infantry concealed in the wood, refused to charge home on the squares, and suddenly turning their horses, retreated at full speed. This disagreeable flight, which filled the whole army with indignation, has been attributed to the bad conduct of one of the officers, who either wanting the skill, or more probably the courage, to execute the movement, fled as fast as he could, and overturning every thing which he met in his passage, carried disorder into the remotest part of our position. As the cuirassiers continued their flight to the rear, they caused the utmost confusion, and struck the bravest hearts with a momentary panic. The camp followers began to pillage the baggage. Some conscripts, who had unwillingly fought in our ranks, contributed to it more than the enemy, to whom this moment of hesitation and alarm afforded no opportunity to gain any decisive success.

Our infantry continued to fight with unabated courage, and in the most perfect order. The chasseurs of the guard, who hastened from Frasné to support them, found their services were scarcely required, and the artillery on our left continued to incommode the English excessively. The firing did not cease until the approach of night, when our troops assumed their position in front of Frasné, after a combat horribly destructive, and equally glorious to both parties. Our loss was estimated at more than four thousand men. That of the English was far greater. The eminences in front of the wood where they arrested our progress, and a hollow road which bordered it, were covered with their dead. Three Scotch regiments and the Brunswick legion were exterminated. Some other corps likewise suffered much. The great number of English officers of rank who fell in this engagement, proves the severity of their loss and the obstinacy of the contest. The Duke of Brunswick perished in this affair.

The author, from whose work the above is extracted, has certainly come as near the truth (with the exception of what relates to the extermination of the three Scotch regiments) as any eye-witness who has attempted to write on the subject; and he being a Frenchman, we must allow him to be possessed of great candour and far from partial.

It is impossible for an individual, who is neither omnipresent nor all-seeing, to give an account of every particular circumstance that takes place on the field of general action, so as to defy contradiction; he must depend in a great measure upon the reports and statements of others regarding what may have occurred at a part of the field remote from his own observation; and in obtaining that which comes nearest the truth, consists the merit of the general writer.

I trust to be the more readily excused for giving an extract from the accounts of one who treats on the general operations of the two armies, as I am not presuming to state on my own authority any thing but what passed within the narrow circle of my own observation, and this I acknowledge to have been so limited, that it seldom extended beyond my own corps.

The day's contest at a close, our attention was directed to the casualties which had occurred in our ranks. We had lost, in killed, one colonel, one lieutenant, one ensign, one sergeant-major, two sergeants, and forty-eight rank-and-file. One brevet lieutenant-colonel, five captains, five lieutenants, two ensigns, fourteen sergeants, one drummer, and two hundred and fourteen rank-and-file composed our list of wounded. Six privates fell into the enemy's hands; among these was a little lad (Smith Fyfe) about five feet high. The French general, on seeing this diminutive looking lad, is said to have lifted him up by the collar or breech and exclaimed to the soldiers who were near him, "Behold the sample of the men of whom you seem afraid!" This lad returned a few days afterwards, dressed in the clothing of a French grenadier, and was saluted by the name of Napoleon, which he retained until he was discharged.

The night passed off in silence: no fires were lit; every man lay down in rear of his arms, and silence was enjoined for the night. Round us lay the dying and the dead, the latter not yet interred, and many of the former, wishing to breathe their last where they fell, slept to death with their heads on the same pillow on which those who had to toil through the future fortunes of the field reposed.

Hail, welcome night! thy pleasant shade woos our wearied limbs to repose, and gives a momentary respite to the contending hosts; withhold thy chilling dews from our uncovered brows; spread thy murky mantle in mildness around our wounded and dying companions; renovate with refreshing sleep our bodily powers, that we may rise in strength for the toil of battle!. Ye spirits of the brave, that hover round this scene of slaughter, be near your surviving comrades, who must yet strive for glory! Look upon us in the moments when victory hesitates, and inspire us to emulate your actions, that our efforts may prove glorious in the success of our country's arms and the achievement of Europe's independence!

CHAPTER 13

Waterloo

On the morning of the 17th the unclouded heavens began to present the approach of day, our usual signal to rise from our sky-canopied bed; but fatigued by our yesterday's march and field movements, we were feasting our wearied limbs, if I may use the expression, and rejoicing in the indulgence of undisturbed repose; but no sooner did twilight enable us to distinguish different fields, or grain from grass, than we started to arms and took up a new line on the field, facing our yet silent foe. Here, after arranging our ranks and equalizing the companies, we piled our arms and commenced to prepare our yesterday's dinner, which served us for an excellent breakfast.

The men not thus engaged were now busily employed in burying the dead, and those who had been attending the wounded in the adjoining houses had not neglected the interest of their respective messes. Besides our own allowances of meat which we bad brought from Brussels, there was not a mess without a turkey, goose, duck, or fowl floating in the seething kettle; and an abundance of vegetables from the neighbouring gardens helped to add to the richness of the soup, which was preparing, and which we got good time to take, and for this we were truly thankful, for we were very hungry.

It would have afforded a little amusement to those accustomed to the attendance of tidy waiters at their well-served tables, to have seen us sitting on our knapsacks round the camp-kettles, lifting up the meat on the point of a bayonet and dividing it without knife or fork; one tearing off the leg of a fowl and handing it to his neighbour; another with a piece of meat, half done, on the point of his ramrod, holding it to the blazing fire. We had now got our craving appetites well satisfied, and we had a sufficiency of beverage to make us comfortable and in good spirits.

Our advanced picquets had occupied, during the night, the fields beyond that on which we had been engaged, and were not yet withdrawn.

A passing fog hung over the plain a short time, but soon disappeared, and left us with a cloudless sky. A general retrograde movement now took place, and we retired on the main road by which we had advanced from Brussels.

It was with regret that many of us left that field, on which some of our men lay breathing their last. Among this number was a young man whose wound was in his forehead, from which the brain protruded; in this state he had lain on the field during the night; his eyes were open, with a death-film over them; two of his comrades were watching the last throb of his expiring breath, before they would consign his body to the grave, already opened to receive it, when the call to arms made us leave him on the field to the hands of strangers.

The sun shone brightly on our arms as we left the fields of Quatre Bras, and passed the farm round which the remains of some thousands of brave men, British, Brunswick, Belgic, and French, were interred; and many yet lay scattered over the fields, and may have remained hidden amidst the grain which still continued standing, until the sickle or the scythe laid the fields bare.

We passed through the small village of Quatre Bras, the houses of which were crowded with our wounded men, whose groans bore testimony to the pain they were suffering as they were about to be conveyed to Brussels. At the same time there were not a few stragglers actively employed searching for pillage, under the pretence of looking for a drink of water.

The enemy did not as yet seem to notice our move-ment, and we continued our march until we had passed the village, half-way to Waterloo. Here we turned off the road to our right, formed in columns, and halted; and short as that halt was, it afforded time for one of our regiments to hold a drumhead court-martial and carry the sentence into effect on the spot. Examples of this kind are absolutely necessary, whatever philanthropists may say to the con-trary; they tend to preserve regularity, order, and discipline; and although an individual may suffer a punishment which is debasing and cruel, yet it is better that this should be awarded and inflicted, than to see hundreds fall victims to the rapacity that might ensue from not timely visiting the aggressor with punishment.

When one outrage is passed over, another must be over-looked, until crimes increase, and we look among those who may be afterwards arraigned and ask ourselves, what have these men done that they should be held up as a public ex-ample more particularly than others who have been guilty of similar delinquencies? Thus at last crime is softened down to delinquency; we become no better than public robbers, perhaps worse, and the poor, oppressed, ruined peasant looks around him for a protector, and finds he has none.

The enemy's guns began now to thunder in our rear, and the sun, which had hitherto shone brightly on our arms, hid his face in thick rolling clouds, as if ashamed to see Britain's sons leave the field to a rebel foe. The very heavens indi-cated anger, as if the ascending spirits of our fallen compan-ions were imploring the ethereal powers to hurl the bolts of their vengeance in our face, to brand us with cowardice, and threaten us with instant destruction for thus basely leaving a field stamped with victory. Loud thunder shook the earth; the clouds, bursting, poured down their accumulated stores on our unsheltered heads; the lightning played on our bayonets; the road became the channel of a river, and the fields on ei-ther side an extensive swamp.

We had now attained the undulating height of Mount St. Jean, and Wellington said "We shall retire no further." The thunder ceased to roll its awful peals through the heavens, the thick embodied clouds deployed, spread wide, and half dissolved in drizzly mist; but as if doubtful of man's resolves, resumed again their threatening aspect, as if to secure our halt.

Our lines now formed behind the long extended ridge of Mount St. Jean, having the village of Waterloo a mile or two in our rear, and at no less a distance the dark forest of Soignes, which extends to Brussels. The right of our front British line extended beyond Hougoumont as far as Braine l'Alleud; the left is said to have extended to Wavre.

Sir T. Picton's division consisted of the 28th, 32nd, 79th, and the 95th (rifle corps), under the command of Sir James Kemp. And the 1st, 42nd, 44th, and 92nd regiments, under the command of Sir Denis Pack, extended from the left of the Brussels road to a copse on a rising ground which probably overlooked the whole field. The extensive farmhouse and offices of La Hay Saint was to the right of the division, but in front and on the right side of the road.

Before us was a line of Belgic and Dutch troops; a narrow road, lined with stunted quickset hedges, runs between this line of foreigners (or I may with more justice say, natives) and us. This road commands a view of the enemy's position, and the side next to us is the artillery's post; the hedges in front form a feeble cover from the enemy's view, but no defence against his shot, shell, or musketry; yet here the gunners stand in all their pride in front of their countrymen, to give a bright example of coolness, courage, and unparalleled perseverance throughout the toils of the following day.

Our line, being on the slope next to Waterloo, was hidden from the enemy, who took up his position on the heights of La Belle Alliance, parallel to those of St. Jean: a valley, corresponding to those wavy heights on either side, divides the two armies, a distance of about half a musket-shot intervening between the adverse fronts. Several lines of British were drawn up further in rear, and several columns seemed to bivouac in the wood near Waterloo.

Being all arranged in the manner pointed out by our immortal leader, we piled our arms, kindled fires, and stood round the welcome blaze to warm ourselves and dry our dripping clothes.

Midnight approached, and all the fields towards the artillery's post were hid in darkness, save what the fitful gleams of our fires cast over them. Silence prevailed, and wet although we were, we were falling asleep sitting round the fires, or stretched on scattered branches brought for fuel. At this time a very heavy shower poured down upon us, and occasioned some movement or noisy murmur in the French army or line of Belgians; this induced our sentries to give an alarm. In an instant each man of the brigade stood by his musket; the bayonets were already on the pieces, and these all loaded, notwithstanding the rain.

We stood thus to our arms for nearly an hour, sinking to our ankles amongst the soft muddy soil of the field, when the alarm was found to be false, and we again sat or lay down to repose.

Oh! how pleasant is rest to the wearied soldier, after a disastrous day's fatigue, and what he deems a retreat! But rest is here denied, the heavens and the earth refuse it. The former pours down its wrath upon our heads, while the latter opens its bosom to give a miry grave.

Long looked for day at last began to break: we stood to our useless arms for a few minutes, and then began to examine their contents. The powder was moistened in the piece and completely washed out of the pan. The shots were drawn, muskets sponged out, locks oiled, and every thing put to rights.

During the night the great Napoleon had joined his elated army, and doubtless about that time when the false alarm roused us to arms, had been the time that his hosts welcomed him to the field, or that he had issued his address to them on the subject of their former victories, in which they had so conspicuously shone. Night had passed over their heads no less uncomfortably than with ourselves, but the charm of Napoleon's presence gave an *eclat* to their busy preparations, more particularly so to those generals who surrounded him in the full pride of already conferred and yet expected honours, while he addressed them briefly on the glories of Friedland, Wagram, Jena, Eylau, and Austerlitz.

Had the sun arisen over the fields in brightness, he would have been welcomed by Napoleon as at Austerlitz; but thick clouds hovered around and veiled that glorious luminary from the view of his devoted army, and he stood himself the sun of his mighty host on the morning of approaching battle, and his praise was shouted from rank to rank. But those shouts died away before reaching our ears; an Almighty Power hushed them in the breathless air.

Now, on our right, Napoleon urged on his heavy columns, while a like movement was made against our left. The guns opened their war-breathing mouths in thundering peals, and all along the ridge of Mount St. Jean arose one dense cloud of smoke.

France now pushed forward on the line of our Belgic allies, drove them from their post, and rolled them in one promiscuous mass of confusion through the ranks of our brigade, which instantly advanced to repel the pursuers, who came pushing on in broken disorder, in the eagerness of pursuit, till obstructed by the hedge and narrow road, while a like obstruction presented itself to us on the other side.

We might have forced ourselves through as the Belgians had done, but our bare thighs had no protection from the piercing thorns; and doubtless those runaways had more wisdom in shunning death, though at the hazard of laceration, than we would have shown in rushing forward upon it in disorder, with self-inflicted torture. The foe beheld our front and paused; a sudden terror seized his flushed ranks. We were in the act of breaking through the hedge, when our general gave orders to open, our ranks. In an instant our cavalry

175

passed through, leaped both hedges, and plunged on the panic-stricken foe. "Scotland forever!" bursts from the mouth of each Highlander, as the Scots Greys pass through our ranks.

What pen can describe the scene? Horses' hoofs sinking in men's breasts, breaking bones and pressing out their bowels. Riders' swords streaming in blood, waving over their heads and descending in deadly vengeance. Stroke follows stroke, like the turning of a flail in the hand of a dexterous thresher; the living stream gushes red from the ghastly wound, spouts in the victor's face, and stains him with brains and blood. There the piercing shrieks and dying groans; here the loud cheering of an exulting army, animating the slayers to deeds of signal vengeance upon a daring foe. Such is the music of the field! Neither drum nor fife is here to mock us with useless din, but guns and muskets raise their dreadful voice, throw out the messengers of death to check a valiant foe, and bid him turn before the more revolting shock of steel to steel ensues. It was a scene of vehement destruction, yells and shrieks, wounds and death; and the bodies of the dead served as pillows for the dying.

And here, brave Picton, our gallant general, thou seest thy heavy squadrons sweep all before them, and in this bright moment of England's glory thou fallest. But thou hast fallen among the brave; Ponsonby rests in death on the field, and Uxbridge honours the ground with his blood.

The guns cease their thundering peals; the infantry gaze in silent wonder at the indiscriminate work of slaughter before them, till, flushed with victory and bathed in blood, the victors drive beyond the bounds of well-timed support, and their bravest lie stretched on those whom their swords have laid low.

Return, ye champions of the field! Return: the trumpet's voice summons you back, and your countrymen anxiously look for the issue.

A thousand prisoners are driven in before our cavalry as they return over the corpse-strewn field, and the loud shouts of ten thousand soldiers welcome the victors back. But long and loud are the enthusiastic cheers of the proud Highlanders as they greet the gallant Greys' approach. "Glory of Scotland!" bursts spontaneously from the mouth of each Highlander, while rending shouts of "England's" or "Ireland's" glory welcomes the 1st and Enniskillen Dragoons, and echoes along the lines.

This dreadful charge made by our cavalry, in our immediate front, gave an impulse bordering on enthusiasm to our spirits that nothing could depress. But the enemy, as if dreading more than common opposition at this spot, forbore to press upon it during the remaining part of the day.

Meanwhile that our heavy dragoons thus bore down all opposition on the left, the enemy was bearing all before him and sweeping the field on the right, until stopped by squares of infantry, and rolled back in confusion on his own supporting columns, followed by our cavalry in turn. The victors and the vanquished appeared, occasionally, like the flight of birds in the northern valleys when the face of the fields is covered with snow; they fly from the forest to the farm, and from the farm to the forest, and no place of rest seems to be theirs. Thus toiled both armies through the day, and the guns never ceased their dreadful roar, save amidst some slaughtering charge, when sword or bayonet did the work of destruction.

The right and left both sustained the impetuous onset of Napoleon's cavalry, and these on each occasion met with powerful opposition, and were driven back in wild confusion. But on the right and centre he seems to urge his greatest force throughout the whole day. La Hay Saint is one pool of blood; against it Napoleon's artillery incessantly play, and columns of infantry are urged on to drive the brave defenders out. But these meet them with fire and steel, and repel them with determined resolution. Here a never ceasing combat rages throughout the day, and forms an interesting object in the general picture of the field.

Hougoumont is no less a scene of slaughter; there every effort is made to obtain possession and to break in upon our right wing. Sometimes in the heat of a charge they rush past its bounds, but meet with wounds or death as they fly back; for it is only when the enemy occasionally pursues his apparently victorious course beyond his lines and past our guns that he gets a view of our columns or lines of infantry, which immediately take advantage of his disordered front, and drive him back with immense loss, beyond our guns and down the descent: they then retire to their well chosen ground and send out a company or two of skirmishers from each regiment to keep up a never ceasing fire, save when driven back on their respective columns in those repeated charges.

That man who brands our foe with cowardice deserves the lie; he advances to our cannon's mouth, and seeks death from the destructive bayonet; but he meets with men inured to war, animated with an equal share of national pride, confident in the success of their leader, and thus rejoicing in the ambitious strife, protract the raging fight.

Hither, ye sage philanthropists, approach and see the battle-field; see man to man a human butcher made, the more he slays the braver man is he!

The sun, as he hastens down, bursts through the hazy clouds and gleams in brightness over the long contested field. It is the setting sun of Napoleon's greatness. No more shall he hail the first rays of that glorious orb as a signal for battle and victory.

The contest still rages, and Wellington's reserves advance to the front. The cannon still throw their death-commissioned charges over the contested ground, and thunder along the ridge of Mount St. Jean.

Towards Brussels, thousands of fugitives, prisoners, horses, mules, and wagons with baggage, roll along without order, and pressing on the bleeding victims of the day, crush them to death or hurry them off the way.

The approach of the fugitives, and the confused appearance of our light baggage, struck Brussels with alarm: the living tide rolled in at its gates, and the early fugitives of the day declared that all was lost; while every succeeding runaway confirmed the unwelcome tidings, to cover his own cowardly flight. The walls were crowded with the anxious inhabitants of the city, as well as with the deeply interested peasantry, who had fled from the scene of action, listening to the hostile report of the guns. Imagination brought the sound at times louder, and as if approaching nearer to their gates; but now when the stream of fugitives poured in, all was confusion and despair. Some fled for safety towards Ghent, Ostend, or Antwerp, while others withdrew to their houses and trusted to the simple security of their bolted doors.

What thoughts may we suppose agitated the breast of our noble leader as his last reserve stood in extended line on the ridge of the heights; when the hydra of France threw forward its heads of battalions to the mouth of our guns? The word was given to charge.

From right to left the welcome word flew over the field; the forest of Soignes echoed to its farthest bounds the loud shouts of an elated army. The guns cease their thundering roar; Brussels hears no more their sound, thinks Britain's cause is lost, and dread despair hangs over its peopled walls. Proud city, fear not! The charge is given from right to left, and all Napoleon's columns and lines, foot and horse, in one mingled mass of confusion, fly over the field, while on our left the hardy Prussians come in to share the toils of the hard-fought day, and push the disorganized enemy over the face of the country, till midnight gives a respite to the pursuer and the pursued.

On the heights of La Belle Alliance, which France had occupied during the day, our troops took up their bivouac for the night; while the severely wounded, the dying, and the dead rested under the cloudless canopy of heaven, on the sloping sides of the late contested valley, until morning threw its dawning light over the death-strewn fields.

Ah! ye sympathizing friends, approach this scene of carnage! Ye who commiserate the distresses of mankind! Ye who deplore the untimely fate of wretches doomed to death for crimes against the law! Ye who raise your voice to mitigate those wretches' well-merited doom, approach and see the men whose only crime has been to serve their country, maintain its proud pre-eminence in the face of Europe, and crush an ambitious foe, insatiate of blood and thirsting for conquest! See those men, who in obedience to the law have fought and bled, yet here un-pitied die!

The rising sun beheld them full of health, of hope, of cheerful spirits, and in the confidence of success to the arms of their country. The mantle of night now darkens the field of their rest, and every hope of life is fled. Their sense of feeling still exists, and warns them that death is nigh; their bed, the miry ground; thirst intolerable demands a cooling draught; they cry for drink, then listen to hear if any friendly foot approaches; no sound comes to their ears but that of groans and calls for drink. No drink is here unmixed with blood, no friendly foot steps over this gory field, but prowling fiends perhaps may steal along to strip the dead. Death, friendly death, how welcome art thou now!

The loss of the regiment this day was trifling, if compared with that which it sustained on the 16th at Quatre Bras: we had only six men killed; one captain, three lieutenants, and thirty-three rank-and-file wounded.

Brussels, which had been kept in a state of excitement since the night of the 15th, heard the glad tidings of the result of the battle, and the doors were opened wide for the reception of the bleeding soldiers, who had been conveyed thither on wagons or had dragged their maimed limbs along the way without assistance.

The poor women, who had been forced back to the rear of the army when the battle commenced, were hurried amidst the mingled mass of fugitives, panic-struck batmen, mules, horses, and cattle, back to the gates of Brussels; but on entering, found no friendly hand stretched out to take them off the streets. Everyone there was full of her own misery, no one had a word of consolation to offer a stranger, and the shade of night was spreading over the ill-foreboding city, as the glad tidings burst from the walls to palaces and streets, until tower and cottage echoed to the joyful bursts of the rejoicing multitude. St. Guidel's bells gave to the passing breeze their joyful peals to animate a desponding country, while every heart was filled with gladness, and every voice shouted out "England and Wellington!"

But amidst this scene of Brussels' joy, there were some who could not participate in the general ebullition of gladness. These were the fugitives, who, witnessing the first successful charge of Napoleon's cavalry, thought all was lost, and sought refuge beyond the range of shot and shell, and left the field to men of stronger nerves. Those runaways, convinced too late of their own demerit, now wished the walls to fall upon them and hide them under their ruins. To return to the field was eternal disgrace; to seek shelter elsewhere, misery.

A few, far different from these, stood oppressed with anxiety, strangers to the scenes of rejoicing or to the voice of gladness that rung from house to house in their ears; these were the poor distressed women who knew not yet of their husbands' fate. To advance through the forest by night, and on a road they had so lately traced, marked with confusion, blocked with overturned baggage, helpless wounded soldiers, and, worst of all, by prowling stragglers, would have been madness. There was no resource but to seek shelter under some hospitable roof; and what city could boast of more hospitality than Brussels, when anxious fears for her own safety were allayed? Each door was opened, and each matron, to whom application was made, gave a British soldier's wife a ready welcome.

Hail, blessed night! Thou art as welcome to the victorious soldier as rest is to the weary traveller, and thy grateful shade gives to his toils a momentary respite, while deeply immersed in sleep he dreams of all his bygone dangers, and thinks that years have passed since the bloody fray, and that he now sits beside the cheerful hearth, telling the wondrous tale to the listening villagers, while their little urchins cling round his knee and think him a great man: so at least he imagines; till starting in the midst of his supposed narration, he finds himself cold and cheerless on the battle-field.

Ye near relations of those who are stretched lifeless on this field of Europe's freedom, of Britain's glory, does sleep hover round the pillow of your repose? or do you watch the mail's arrival to hear accounts from the scene of hostilities? or do you meditate the despatch of letters to relations or friends engaged in this campaign? Soon, very soon, shall the joyful post appear with the glorious tidings of victory to the arms of Britain, but gloomy tidings he brings to you whose friends lie slain on the field of battle. No answer shall be returned to your letter, except from the hand of a friendly stranger. Your friend lies cold on the field, surrounded with the gory dead; perhaps the vital spark is struggling to quit its painful prison, and seek a more welcome abode in happier regions, far from war and strife, "where the troublers cease to give annoyance, and the weary rest."

Night passes over the groaning field of Waterloo, and morning gives its early light to the survivors of the battle to return to the heights of St. Jean, on purpose to succour the wounded or bury the dead.

Here may be seen the dismounted gun, the wheels of the carriage half sunk in the mire; the hand of the gunner rests on the nave, his body half-buried in a pool of blood, and his eyes open to heaven, whither his spirit has already fled.

Here are spread, promiscuously, heaps of mangled bodies—some without head, or arms, or legs—others lie stretched naked, their features betraying no mark of violent suffering.

The population of Brussels, prompted by a justifiable curiosity, approach the field to see the remains of the strangers who fell to save their spoil-devoted city, and to pick up some fragment as a memorial of the battle, or as a relic for other days. Of these the field affords an abundant harvest: *cuirasses*, helmets, medals, swords, pistols, and all the various weapons of destruction in military use, besides the balls and bullets, which may be ploughed up a thousand years hence. Here also are hundreds of blankets, ripped up knapsacks, torn shirts, stockings, and all the simple contents of the fallen soldiers' kits. Letters and memoranda of the slain strew the field in every direction, which are picked up by the curious and carefully preserved.

Giraud, from whose work I made free to make an extract regarding the operations of Quatre Bras, remarks, in his closing account of the battle of Waterloo, that:

> Such were the principal circumstances, and such the issue of the battle of Mont St. Jean (Waterloo), which would have resembled the disasters of Poictiers, of Cressy, of Agincourt, and of Pavia, if, by inflicting so fatal a blow on our military power, it had not produced a compensation for our reverses, in the return of a monarch from whom the nation anxiously expects the termination of its misfortunes.

> History will not withhold the meed of praise which is due to the victims of the ambition of this terrific madman, whom she will rank with Genghis-Khan or with Tamerlane. She will say, that if valour alone could have secured the victory, the French army would have been invincible.

The French writers attribute the loss of the battle to some fatal errors committed by Napoleon, particularly in his obstinate neglect of Marshal Grouchy's disposition, and putting all to the hazard of bearing down our centre, so near the close of the day. But it must be considered, that if the enemy had been victors, all those retrospective errors would have been magnified into well-digested plans which none but the master-mind of the great Napoleon could have been capable of unfolding. His obstinacy would have been considered firmness and courage, blended with an implicit confidence in the bravery of his troops and the talents of his generals. His neglect of the Prussians, whom he supposed Grouchy was watching or pursuing, would have been ascribed to a contempt of their abilities to out-manoeuvre him. In short, there would have been no errors or misconduct, but each operation naturally producing its intended effect, finally leading to the annihilation of the opposing armies, and the glory of France.

CHAPTER 14

Homewards

The din of battle has ceased on the plain. The sun has attained the meridian. The bugles call again to arms, and the martial life-stirring pipes give their wild wailings to the plaided sons of Caledonia, and gather them from the graves of their comrades to advance after the retreating foe.

An appearance of cleanly comfort, notwithstanding the late distracted state of the country, seems to prevail over the face of the Netherlands, where considerable respect is paid by the army to the property of the inhabitants, and our march is confined to the main or cross roads by which we advance. The weather was pleasant, though somewhat sultry; and we halted, by the orders of the general, in columns on the road or fields adjoining, for a few minutes, each successive hour.

The Scotch Greys were enjoying one of those rests, which proved so refreshing to every corps on the line of march, and our brigade, after having enjoyed a similar one in rear, was marching past them. A sudden halt was made, whether by order or a natural impulse of national feeling, I know not; but a loud cheering commenced from both sides, and a mutual break of the ranks took place, until an interchange of canteens and spirit horns, pledged to reciprocal friendship and "Auld lang syne," shut our vociferous mouths for some seconds, after which a shaking of hands and loud cheering commenced, and we parted as much elated as on the day of Waterloo, when they passed through our ranks to battle and victory.

We continued our route through Mons, and entered the French frontiers at Malplaquet, the site of one of Marlborough's glorious victories.

We are now on enemy's ground, and the relentless Prussians are desolating in front. We find the houses stripped of their furniture; the china-ware, glasses, mirrors, chimney-ornaments, broken and scattered about in fragments; the statues and busts of eminent persons cast from their pedestals and dashed to pieces. The fields, on which the victors have rested, are spread with beds, blankets, torn carpets, linen, and tapestry. All sorts of furniture and utensils, mixed in wild wasting disorder, present themselves to our view, leaving a sad memorial to the distressed peasantry of Prussia's retaliation for the insults and outrages suffered by her from France.

Indeed, the march of the Prussians might be well compared to that of the Goths after the death of Fritigern. "Their mischievous disposition," says the historian, "was shown in the destruction of every object which they wanted strength to remove or taste to enjoy."

I have no doubt but the same character might have been as applicable to us, had our country suffered similar injuries to those which Prussia had sustained from the French; and had we been permitted to act without control.

It was no small advantage to us that those vindictive troops had taken the advance, notwithstanding that no houses were left un-sacked in their rear. The gardens and fields were offering their earliest productions to our hand. The potatoes were in full blossom, and the roots, though small, were tempting to lift, and to us a desirable but forbidden prize. Our officer commanding interdicted us from taking that liberty with the fields and gardens which the Prussians had taken with the houses; and it was at the risk of corporal punishment that a soldier could help his mess to a few vegetables from the garden of a deserted house.

We halted one day in the close vicinity of a deserted village, about a mile or two beyond a river (perhaps the Somme). This village consists of two rows of houses, one on each side of the road; that to the right of the road has a range of neat gardens, lined with well-dressed hedges; and in the separating fences, between the different properties, there were small wickets at which we could pass out of the one garden into the other, as if there had been a community of interest amongst the proprietors, or at least a very good understanding amongst them.

There is an extensive belt of wood at a small distance, and it almost encircles the village fields. Here the houses were completely gutted; the apothecary's mortars and pestles, gallipots, phials, and drugs were strewed about his little laboratory; the doors were wrenched from the posts and cast down, to serve as a couch for some one less, fortunate than his neighbour in seizing a mattress or a feather-bed.

A few of our men had made free to enter the gardens, along the fences of which our tents were pitched, and were returning with vegetables for their respective messes, when they were met by our officer commanding, who ordered them off to the rear-guard; fortunately for them, General Pack was passing, and he, after hearing the case, gave great satisfaction to all, no doubt to the very officer who had ordered the arrest, by releasing the prisoners, and setting the matter at rest regarding the supplying the wants of the camp from the enemy's fields.

This decision having been made in favour of the soldiers, the gardens were in a short space cropped of every culinary article, and left as bare as if a swarm of locusts had eaten up every green blade and berry. For, thus licensed, the currant berries were pulled from the bending bushes, the ripe cherries from the overloaded trees, and the green peas and beans became good booty, and open to all.

Indulgences of this kind, however, are seldom granted without giving room for abuses, the recapitulation of which might be as uninteresting as uncalled for; and if some traits of generosity were occasionally blended with outrages, the latter too often so far exceeded the other as to leave no room to consider any of those traits as inherent virtues or national vices peculiar to the country to which the individuals who bore a share in those acts laid claim.

This village having been abandoned by the principal part of its inhabitants, it was supposed by some that they had taken refuge with some of their most valuable effects in the wood, and as soon as the tents were pitched, not a few of our men directed their unauthorized course thither, some under pretence of procuring wood for fuel, or for erecting temporary huts for the night, but with the real intention of obtaining *booty.*

Two or three of these stragglers, for a soldier seldom or never attempted singly a distant enterprise, having espied an ass browsing under a tree, one of them (a married man whose wife was following in rear of the army) thought this a valuable prize, and accordingly made the capture. He was in the act of leading it off, exulting in his good fortune, when its owner, an old man, made his appearance from an adjoining thicket, where he had been concealing himself, and with moving tone and gesture supplicated for the release of his animal.

Age is generally respected, but when it appears amidst misfortunes, not the effects of self-improvidence, struggling with adversity, and the tear of injured feelings trickling down the furrowed cheek, the appeal for support is seldom made in vain. But there are some whose avaricious disposition silences every generous call of manly virtue, and grasps at any thing which promises a present or an anticipated advantage. He who made the capture was one of those callous kind of beings.

The old man's language was not understood, but his supplicating gestures and tears of distress came home to every bosom of the participators in the capture or robbery; yet so far does bad example tend to corrupt and debase those who become exposed to its hardening influence, that they who would act otherwise if otherwise led, consent by silence to that which their hearts despise, and their words at other times condemn.

The animal was about being driven or led off, when the old man's lamentations reached the ears of another party looking out for booty also. Amongst the latter was a young man of whom I may have occasion to make mention hereafter: he was one of those who joined the regiment the preceding year from a French prison, having been a prisoner of war; he not only understood the French language, but spoke it fluently; he heard the poor man's complaint, and represented to his own and the other party the losses he had sustained; he had been turned out of his house, plundered of all worth taking, and what was not worth taking destroyed; he had lost all save this animal, on which he now placed his dependence for earning a livelihood, should he himself survive the misery of the time.

Every voice demanded the restitution, and the disappointed captor was obliged to yield up his prize to its proper owner, who was advised, by the spokesman of the party, to return to the village and resume the occupation of his house, and fear no danger; he did so, met with no opposition, brought his family from their retreat in the wood, and blessed those whom he had occasion at first to curse, not only as the enemies of his country but of himself.

The only privation to which the soldiers were subjected, during their advance to Paris, was an occasional want of water, particularly when marching in the sultry heat of the day along a dusty road: the treading of our feet threw up the dust in suffocating clouds, while the men became parched with thirst, and left their ranks in every direction, whenever a stream, well, pool, or puddle presented itself.

We were indulged with a few minutes' rest every hour, and these halts, intended for refreshment or relaxation, though designed for the benefit of the whole brigade, yet, under certain circumstances, did not serve every regiment alike for that purpose. Some officers in command would not permit the front file of their respective corps to pass up to the rear files of the preceding one, therefore had to rest where halted, when perhaps a stream of water was running past the one in front; and when the brigade resumed the march, it became a very unpleasant duty to keep the men in their ranks; the much-desired object was in view, and there was no resisting the temptation. On these occasions, too frequently, the non-commissioned officers would go, as if for the purpose of bringing back the stragglers, though more with the intention of getting that for themselves of which they were to deprive the privates. The men were thus hurried along, cursing those whose privileged rank allowed them that enjoyment which they, the inferiors, were denied.

On or about the 1st of July, we were approaching a small village; the wind blew the dust in suffocating clouds, no water appeared on either side of the road, and many of the men lay down unable or unwilling to proceed one step further. Officers and men suffered alike, but certainly the men who were under the burden of heavy arms, ammunition, and knapsacks, were more to be pitied than those who marched under less encumbrance. After marching what we considered a long day's march, we struck off the main road, which diverged to the left; that by which we proceeded, was a narrow cross road, and led us to the place of our night's encampment.

The officer who then commanded had, during the whole day, been extremely vigilant in keeping the ranks locked up; he had been incessantly riding round the battalion, placing himself on the right flank of the front file and allowing the whole to pass, then galloping up the left, and resuming his post on the right flank. This vigilance, on the part of our commander, was intended to guard against any leaving his ranks.

After quitting the main road, we came to a pleasant valley, watered by a considerable stream; the road lies along the right bank of a water-course or mill-lead. Nothing could now resist the rush that was made towards the water, and to have made a formal halt would have detained the following regiment, as eager for the enjoyment as ourselves: the self-deniers therefore marched on, while those impelled by the irresistible call of thirst gratified it, though under a threat of punishment; but the number of those brought with us into the field was so few, and of the disobedient left behind so many, that an example of severity was not resorted to; the delinquents of course were forgiven, and the trespass forgotten.

It is to he observed, that by yielding to a craving inclination to drink, we stimulate a flame that demands incessant quenching, and the more we attempt to keep it under by pouring water upon it, the more it is excited to blaze forth; it must be smothered, not slaked; by self-denial and short endurance thirst can be overcome, and the man who firmly denies himself the indulgence of drink for a few days, will easily extend his abstinence to weeks, months, and even years. I do not suggest that system of self-denial for another which I myself have not observed; years have elapsed since the occurrence before mentioned took place, and I am not ashamed to say, without considering it egotism, that from that day forwards, during my service, water never passed my throat; and when on the march it became my duty to prevent men quitting their ranks to drink, I could with the better grace, and without meeting with a sulky look or reply, endeavour to persuade them to bear with their suffering. I recommend this observation more particularly to a non-commissioned officer than to a private; the latter has only his own conduct to answer for, the former has not only his own but that of the other, in a general sense of duty, to account for.

On the 4th July we encamped on the right bank of the Seine, at Clichy, near Paris, and for ten weeks the produce of the gardens, vineyards, orchards, and fields were free to our hands; but this freedom being abused, was withdrawn, yet not until little remained for use; and by that time public confidence was so far restored, that our camp was well supplied with every necessary of life; our pay was regular and our rations good.

Contiguous to the camp was a small island thickly covered with willow trees, and thousands of young saplings, rising from the parent roots, sprung up to a great height: these afforded excellent materials for constructing huts, and the leisure hours of those who had wives were devoted to the erecting of sheds, similar to those we had constructed in former campaigns: they not only afforded a cooler retreat in summer than the tents, but protected us more effectually from cold and rain.

It is with satisfaction I bring to my recollection how pleasantly I was then situated. My little hut, small as it was, I thought enviable; behind it gently flowed the Seine; before it rose a green bank; a little arched porch of wicker-work guarded my feeble door, of plaited twigs, from casual gusts of wind. The interior was about eight feet long and six wide, and decorated with some paltry gewgaws obtained from some of the scattered wreck of the deserted mansions in the neighbourhood. A little *link* or seat of turf ran along the side of the bed, and this was the only place where we could sit, and we used it as our sofa. One pane of glass gave ample light to the interior, where, among the puerile ornaments with which female fancy liked to deck the wicker frame, were strings, and clusters of cut glass, the wreck of Jerome Bonaparte's splendid chandeliers, which had been dashed in pieces and scattered over the floors of his deserted chateau.

From this description of my habitation, of which I was proud, some may conclude that it was miserable enough, but to me it was of no small importance, and its respectability was only to be known by the appearance it had when compared with those which rose up around it. The reader may smile at the idea of such respectability, but I really thought it respectable, and was satisfied with the comforts it afforded. What Goldsmith says of the Swiss peasant's lot, might have been justly applied to mine:

> *Though poor the peasant's hut, his feast though small,*
> *He sees his little lot, the lot of all;*
> *Sees no contiguous palace rear its head*
> *To shame the meanness of his humble shed.*

The regiment began to recruit its strength again, by the joining of our men from Brussels and Antwerp, where the military hospitals had been established. Colonel (now Sir Robert H.) Dick, having so far recovered as to be considered convalescent, resumed the command of the regiment, and, I may say, re-organized it.

Our field exercise was easy, and regularly over between seven and eight every morning. We had then the whole day for amusement, for regular breakfast messes had not then gained a footing in the regiment, that meal, if it could be called one, was a *shift off:* a bit of bread, and the morning allowance of spirits, satisfied the greater number better than they are now, when a system is enforced to sit down to breakfast at the sound of drum or bugle. Neither had we any roll-calls for dinner; if a man did not think proper to attend, he might absent himself without being called to account: but he had no redress or compensation for the loss of his mess, if it was not laid aside for him by his comrade; and we heard of no complaints or grumbles afterwards.

The man who is occasionally accustomed to plenty and to want, submits with less inconvenience to the latter, when he is obliged to do so; and it may perhaps be found that over much attention to our comforts, instead of proving an individual advantage, may turn out a national evil.

Twelve weeks passed pleasantly over in this delightful place. October was approaching with its cloudy sky, and the trodden fields were presenting their bleak, neglected appearance, when we struck camp and proceeded to take up winter-quarters. Some careless or ill-intentioned wretch set fire to our huts as the long roll of the drum and sound of the bagpipe called us to get into the ranks, and with regret I looked back on the rising smoke of our own huts, and forward on the rising flames of those of another regiment, among the beautiful trees that lined the bordering grounds of Clichy. This was a most wanton outrage, and was reprobated by everyone, perhaps even by the unknown incendiary himself, when he saw the branches of the tall trees catching the flame.

We halted one night at St. Germain, a town beautifully situated on the brow of an upland overlooking the mazy windings of the Seine, as it passes through one of the loveliest valleys of which France can boast; and although autumn's golden hue began to grow faint on the bordering heights, still the lingering remains of summer beauty played on the face of the fields and retained the reluctant leaves on the fading boughs. Here is an extensive park or royal forest, once the favourite resort of majesty, but now much neglected.

Here is also an ancient palace, in tolerable repair: it was built by Charles the Fifth of France, and was the residence of the last James of England and of his grandson, Prince Charles Edward. One short century has not yet elapsed since kings, queens, lords, and ladies proudly paced through these halls, and now the plaided ranks of Caledonia find shelter under its roof, and in the vestibules light their fires and proceed with their culinary avocations, while some examine well the numerous apartments and gaze around with respectful awe on the ancient heraldic ornaments that decorate the side of the lofty chapel, now yielding to time, and mouldering on the dank blotched walls. And here are some rusty arms, a sad memorial of the last of the Stuarts.

Highlanders! Let these rusty remains be sacred as a memorial of French hospitality to the last of an illustrious race of kings and an unfortunate fallen family.

The two Highland regiments of the brigade having been allotted this old palace for their quarters, the other two regiments were billeted on the inhabitants, who received them kindly, and treated them with a degree of hospitality not expected.

The following day, as we were ready to march off, the whole were detained by order of the general, in consequence of a complaint having been made that one of the soldiers had stolen a pair of scissors, the property of a tailor. Inquiry was made along the ranks; but what soldier would steal such a paltry article, or at least acknowledge having done so?

The general ordered a strict search to be made, and every soldier of the four regiments had to submit his knapsack to a minute inspection, but to no purpose; I even doubt if they were stolen, or if they had, and been found, that the tailor would have acknowledged them, after valuing them at thirty-six francs (about thirty shillings sterling), which was paid by a stoppage of one farthing off each man's pay, and we marched off all honest men, yet, by this accusation and public exposure, every one under the suspicion of being a thief.

We now proceeded to Chateau Neuf, or Neuf-le-Chateau, a delightful village, pleasantly situated on the brow of a hill, overlooking a finely cultivated country, extending towards Versailles and Montford.

Behind the town the hill rises with an easy ascent, covered with a considerable forest of trees, and the fields, which slope down on each side of the village to the plain, are lined with thriving belts of wood.

The regiment remained in Neuf-le-Chateau until the 30th November, when we received orders to proceed to Boulogne for embarkation. We proceeded on our route by Meulun, Pontoise, Beaumont, Nally, Beauvais, Marselle, and Peaux; at each of which we were received with the most hospitable kindness.

On the 2nd December the frost set in with unusual severity: the cold was more like that of the polar regions than of France. Our Highlanders had their flesh laid open and bleeding by the ruffling of the kilts against their thighs; the icicles gathered in clusters at our eyebrows, and the whiskered men appeared as if they had been powdered by some hairdresser; but we had no sickness. We rested two nights in Abbeville, and a fall of snow relaxed the intensity of the cold.

From Abbeville we proceeded to Boulogne, by Newpont, Montreuil, and Samair; and at all these places we were received with the utmost kindness.

On our arrival at Boulogne we were quartered in the suburbs and adjacent villages, in consequence of the transports not having arrived for our embarkation. The day was stormy; sleet and snow fell around us, as we ranged about inquiring for our quarters, from one house to another, and from that to some remote farm or villa, until many, giving up hopes of ever finding a house to admit them, returned to the billet-master, procured another billet, and set out to find another landlord. We were far from ascribing our disappointments to the taciturnity of those to whom we applied for instructions, or as guides, but to our ignorance of the language in which it would have been necessary to address them.

I had been kept wandering about from hamlet to cottage, and from cottage to hamlet, with my poor wife dripping wet, and almost unable to proceed further, yet struggling to get through the miry fields. Having been directed to a small house as our quarters, about a furlong off the road, we proceeded thither.

On approaching the door, the surly peasant denied us entrance. I presented my billet; he looked upon it, and signified by his comprehensive gestures that we had to go over a few fields before we could reach the place mentioned in it. At this time the snow was falling so thick, we could not see the house towards which he. pointed. However, not to be putting off time uselessly disputing about bad quarters, we proceeded, and, after passing over a few ridges, came to a fortified building, regularly walled and *fossed*.

I passed a drawbridge and stood, a most sorry figure indeed, knocking at the entrance; but this was disregarded, for no one appeared to admit or challenge me, and the place seemed more like a deserted military station than a marching soldier's quarters. I therefore returned disappointed and angry, my poor companion tired and vexed, to the cottage from which I had been directed; entered, and, throwing off my knapsack, desired my wife to consider this our quarters, and see after getting her clothes dried.

The landlord became clamorous, and by passionate words and gestures strove to convince me that I could not be accommodated; but, as I was well convinced of some other one than myself being wrong, by the manner in which I had been kept ranging about, I was determined not to comprehend one word, sign, or gesture of my host, and ordered, as I best could, fuel for the hearth; this he refused, or did not comprehend; I therefore, without much ceremony, served myself with a few billets of wood.

Meantime a messenger had been despatched to a small village, a few furlongs off, for a person to settle concerning my taking possession. On this person's arrival he was presented with the billet, upon which he seemed to reason with my landlord as if I had a right to be admitted; and after a short conversation aside, the stranger turned to me, and in good English requested me to follow him; I packed up and accompanied him to the village, where I was comfortably quartered in a respectable small tavern. From this I had to return to the guard-house and apprize the orderly-man of my company where I was billeted; for it was a rule, when on the march, or in cantonments, to have a man of each company in waiting at the guard, so as to be in readiness to go for the orderly-sergeant of his company in the event of being required.

This being all settled, and the companies so widely scattered about, I made myself certain of not being required for any regimental purpose that night. I flattered myself falsely. I was about retiring to bed, when the orderly-man made his appearance, desiring my attendance at the quarters of the assistant sergeant-major*. The poor lad was covered with mire to the knees, his bonnet was like the wings of a drowned raven, and his clothes and appointments were the same as if he had passed through the English Channel. I accompanied him to the place where the sergeants were to assemble, and after waiting some time, one of the sergeants observed:

---

* The full sergeant-major (now quartermaster) was quartered at a distance of nearly two miles from Boulogne.

"There must be something particular to communicate when we are thus kept waiting, after being brought from such a distance and at so late an hour."

"The orders may be particular," said a second, "but not express, otherwise we should not be detained in this manner waiting for them."

A third (M'Leod) added, "I'll be d—d if I wait five minutes longer for any man born."

Accordingly he departed, and in a few seconds afterwards the assistant sergeant-major made his appearance; of course M'Leod was absent, and called to account next morning. A difference existed between the two, and more angry feelings were excited; both were obstinate; M'Leod was put under arrest, from which he was not relieved until the arrival of the regiment at Hythe: there he was tried by a court-martial, and acquitted for want of sufficient evidence to substantiate the charges*.

From that time his disposition became refractory, and he stood at bay on the most trifling points of duty: indeed, to recapitulate the different quarrels, misunderstanding, and disagreements between him and the other, who had been the cause of that trial; his reducements, his re-appointments, and disappointments, until he became the taker up of other men's grievances, would occupy more pages than the limits of these sketches can admit. It may be enough to add, that he was at last discharged from the regiment, and if with a character, an indifferent one—if with a pension, a trifling one, notwithstanding his having served about seventeen years; and until the time when these cross purposes took place, he was considered an exemplary soldier, brave in the field, of

---

* M'Leod was tried for being absent when the orders were issued, and for contemptuous language to the assistant sergeant-major; but as there was no evidence to support the latter charge, but the prosecutor's, and M'Leod denying it, the case was dismissed. M'Leod called for the proceedings of this court-martial afterwards, in order to repudiate the evidence of the same individual on one of his after-trials, but they could not be found.

orderly and peaceable conduct in camp and in quarters: his personal appearance was good; lie stood upwards of six feet four inches in height.

Now, the purport of the orders, for which we were thus called to have communicated to us, was of so trivial a nature, that it is not to be supposed the commanding-officer would have caused the immediate delivery, considering the manner in which we were distributed through the country; and the issuing of them by no means affected the acceleration or the postponement of any duty or movement. All that was communicated was—that in consequence of the transports not having arrived at Boulogne, the regiment was to proceed to Calais for embarkation, halting one night at Marquise; and we had been previously apprized, though verbally, that we were to embark at Calais.

Besides, this order did not countermand our assembling at the usual hour of the morning for the march, when, if ordered, we would have been equally as ready to retrograde as to advance. Upon the whole, I considered this call as originating with the assistant sergeant-major, to show off a little of his own importance in the presence of the family on whom he was quartered, or to take the advantage of some of the sergeants for non-attendance.

There is nothing more vexatious in a regiment than the misfortune of having an obstinate, inconsiderate, petulant, overbearing sergeant-major or assistant. Many are the annoyances he can occasion to the non-commissioned officers under him, without ever letting any knowledge of them reach the ear of his commanding-officer; and even if it should, he is daily in his presence, has every opportunity of exonerating himself from blame, and if he does not succeed in inculpating the complainer, he may at least throw a cloud of suspicion around him, and succeed in making a very unfavourable impression on the mind of the commanding-officer, regarding the man who has had the boldness to accuse him.

A sergeant-major has an arduous duty to perform; in all the arrangements of regimental duty, he takes, or ought to take, the most active concern. He has of course been considered by his promoter a meritorious man, before he appointed him to this the highest step to which a non-commissioned officer can attain; and as it is frequently found necessary to consult him on the interior economy of the regiment, if he be possessed of any talents, they are sure to be seen and called forth more and more; while many a private soldier may be possessed of far brighter parts, yet, from not having any opportunity of displaying them, he is looked upon, if not with contempt, at least with cool indifference.

Fortunate is the regiment which possesses a good sergeant-major. His rank is not such as to make him above associating with and advising the non-commissioned officers; his own personal example is the means of swaying all their actions; he cautions them against unjust oppression, yet shrinks not from pointing out the cases which require coercive measures; and where his advice fails of its intended effect, he draws not back from the consequences to the injury of the individual who has acted upon it. He recommends for promotion those who meritoriously aspire to rise from the ranks. His commanding-officer is seldom troubled with complaints, for he settles them to the satisfaction of the accuser and the accused; no mercenary motive actuates his conduct in reconciling differences, and his hands are never stained with the gift of an inferior. He is like the pure mountain-stream, which from inaccessible sources derives its never-failing supply, and sweeps off every thing impure from its channel.

To those who are unacquainted with the influence which sergeant-majors generally possess, this may seem a hyperbole, but to me it appears a fact, and many a non-commissioned officer and private soldier has found it so to his experience. I speak not of one regiment, but of many: he can be a little tyrant in his corps, without the knowledge of the commanding-officer; the same as a pay-sergeant may be in a company, unknown to his captain; his unnecessary acts of oppression may be made to appear to his superiors laudable zeal, and his severity a merit deserving reward.

This same *acting* sergeant-major's promotion to be sergeant-major, and afterwards adjutant, may show very plainly how a commanding-officer may be biased by a too favourable opinion of an undeserving man. And, I make free to say, that of the very few who rise from the ranks to commissions, not one in twenty recommends himself by his manly merit, but by his cringing servility, his forward impudence, or by watching well the time when he can show off before superiors his authority over men who must obey. Such, generally, are the few who are promoted.

Such partial and ill-discriminated promotions, instead of serving as a stimulus to others, create heart-burnings and carelessness. The fortunate favourite looks down with contempt on those whom he has overstepped, and being intimately acquainted with their merits and their demerits, weaknesses, opinions, and prejudices, fails not to make these serviceable in mortifying such of them he dreaded as rivals.

In time of war there are some chances of a man proving himself deserving by some service of conspicuous merit. In such a case, the man would be undeserving the name of soldier who would grudge him his well-earned honour of reward; but it is no less than a robbing of the country, seeing that commissions are sold to gentlemen, educated and qualified to hold them, to give one to an individual of no influence, and whose only merit may be that of being thought well of by his commanding-officer, and daily in his presence, but still one who perhaps would sell his country, as Esau did his birthright, for a morsel of pottage.

The advocates for promotion from the ranks hold up Napoleon's system of promotion as a pattern for British imitation; but there is a wide difference between the constitution of the British army, as it is, and that of the French, as it was under that great man.

The French army was solely composed of men raised by conscription; the rich and the poor, the learned and the ignorant, were all liable to serve in the ranks; and the army was ever actively employed in trying service, in which the real military talent of every man was brought to public view by what may be called a fair competition. It is not known, moreover, what Napoleon's views might have been regarding promotion, had his active spirit permitted him to rest in peace when he found himself thoroughly established on the throne of the Bourbons. Besides, it would not have been good policy in him to have confined his patronage to the great, who might have considered themselves degraded by submitting to a ruler of meaner ancestry than their own. Thus promotion from the ranks was the consolidation of his power.

In time of peace there must be another criterion whereby to judge of the merit of a candidate for military promotion than that of his commanding-officer's easily biased opinion. And I must add, that soldiers like better to have men of fortune and family influence over them than needy aspirants. From the man of interest the soldier may expect, when the period of his service is expired, and when he is creditably discharged, a recommendation which may be successful in obtaining for him a comfortable situation; such as that of a storekeeper or barrack-sergeant, a police-officer, letter-carrier, porter to one of the public offices, civil or military, the keeper of a lodge, the ranger of a forest, &c, according to the abilities he may be possessed of to enable him to hold any of those situations. The needy man is generally the greedy man, he wants the soldier's service for nothing, and he has so many demands for his own personal advancement, that he cannot or will pot exert himself in behalf of an inferior.

After this unnecessary call and vexatious detention, we were permitted to return to our quarters, and communicate the orders to the officers and men at the time which they should have been given to ourselves, *viz.*, when the regiment assembled in the morning.

Marquise is a small straggling village a few miles from Boulogne; in it we were quartered one night; next day, the 17th of December, we reached Calais and embarked. Our vessels steered for Dover, but that in which my company was on board, meeting with a contrary wind or current, made for Ramsgate; this was the means of keeping us a day longer at sea.

CHAPTER 15

We are Welcomed Home

Government provides amply enough for the accommodation of troops on long voyages; a passage such as this, from Calais to Dover, or to Ramsgate, is not deserving the name of voyage: the distance is so inconsiderable, that the time of performing it can be pretty closely calculated, and accommodation or comfort is not looked for or much regarded by passengers; but in the event of unexpected delays, it becomes the more unpleasant as it is unprovided for.

We look back on the receding shores of that country which we have left, and forward to those for which we are bound; yet the wind drives us back from the latter as we attempt to approach, and the waves repel us from the former as we seem to recede: cold blasts chill our limbs on deck, and the crowded hold emits its sickening, foul, repulsive breath; yet the voice of mirth is there, and the man is best worthy of the world that rejoices in the world and makes the most of it. Let the storm rage around us, we shall descend to the laughter-loving crowd; mirth is more desirable than sorrow; there we shall witness the shouts of merriment that occasionally convulse the throng, even although at our own sea-sick expense.

Here, full of harmless gaiety, sits Kate, the wife of Edward M'Kay; time has not yet put an aged wrinkle-on her brow, and with a pleasant cheerful countenance and handsome person, she is gifted with that readiness of reply for which the sons and daughters of our sister island are so greatly and so justly famed; she sits, the centre of the merry circle; to her the talkative direct their rude witticisms, and her repartees fly back with well-directed aim—to the sweet with sweetness, and to the bitter with bitterness. Kate was what we call an old campaigner; that is, she had seen more than one campaign, and could take her own part with any woman on board. The greenhorns were repulsed by the sharpness of her remarks, and the profane found little to boast of in their profanity by the acrimonious retort it so well merited.

And yonder sit a few together, in pensive silence. This is no fit place for the modest matron or the virtuous wife; but she must submit, without complaining, to her adverse lot.

There is nothing perhaps more unpleasant to a woman of any virtuous principle than that of being so situated, as to be under the necessity of listening to the gross lascivious remarks of vulgar wit, from which she has no opportunity to withdraw herself; for, if she repulses them with scorn after having sanctioned them with a smile, she is accused of cunning, and her female companions, whom perhaps envy or ill-nature prompts to slander, fail not to offer their censorious remarks and insinuations regarding her conduct, when less submitted to observation.

I have heard of a Dutch artist who never drew the interior of a domicile without introducing into his picture a utensil which decent chambermaids keep out of sight; and I might no less trespass upon the delicacy of my reader, were I to enlarge on all the causes of mirth that shake the crowded hold.

Night casts its murky mantle over our troubled path, as our vessel labours to gain the destined port; we look for a place to rest, but in vain; and our disappointment meets with no condolence, but affords cause of more mirth. Thus the hours that fly hastily in our enjoyments, seem to linger in our affliction, and to lengthen our term of uneasiness. The sweet land of our expected repose, however, was not far distant.

We were now approaching Ramsgate, after being two days at sea, and a heavy swell beat along the coast; our sails were lowered, the impulse they had already given the vessel seemed sufficient to carry her into the harbour. The soldiers stood crowded on deck; whether they gave any interruption to the management of the helm or stood in the way of the seamen may be uncertain, but the prow struck on the pier. The shock was like that of an earthquake; the men on deck staggered forward, fell down, or fortunately grasped a rope, as the vessel heeled back on the north side of the pier. Happily the quay was crowded with spectators to witness our debarkation, and by their means we regained the harbour without any loss, landed all in good health, and were received with kindly greetings by the assembled multitude that waited our arrival.

A heavy fall of snow hastened our departure for Sandwich, where we were quartered for the night. We proceeded by Deal and Dover to Hythe, where we lay two weeks refitting ourselves in necessaries and military appointments. From Hythe we marched to Chelmsford, by Ashford, Faversham, Chatham, Gravesend, Brentwood, and Ingatstone.

After being two weeks in Chelmsford Barracks, we took the route for Sunderland, a long march and in an unpleasant season; but such was the reception we met with at every town where we halted, either for an hour or for a night, that although the roads had been as bad as those in Spain, and the weather worse than it happened to be, we would have considered ourselves more than recompensed by the kindly welcome we received from the inhabitants.

The munificent hands of all classes poured in their offerings to fill the cup of cordial kindness that sparkled to our lips at our approach. Without doubt, many of us disappointed the expectation of our generous benefactors, for the gifts bestowed were frequently intended to benefit the landlord on whom we were billeted, and in whose house they were expected to be expended; notwithstanding, they were often devoted to another, and sometimes to another town. An innkeeper may pardon the meanness of a soldier who refuses to expend at his bar that money which a generous patron has given for that purpose; but he cannot be expected to feel pleased by the ungrateful receiver spending it at another, perhaps that of a rival, and then returning intoxicated to claim the privilege of a lodger. If such was done by some, I trust they were the few of the despised number.

We left Chelmsford on the 16th* January, 1816, and were received very kindly at Dunmow and Saffron Walden. The bells of Cambridge welcomed us with joy. Every table smoked with savoury viands for our entertainment, and every cellar contributed a liberal supply of its best October for our refreshment. We were permitted to enter the buildings of the University, and to gratify our curiosity by viewing whatever was worthy of admiration, and, of course, every part of that venerable pile of buildings is deserving the regard of the visitor. We were also presented with a donation equal to two day's pay to each man.

On approaching Huntingdon, a halt was made at the request of a gentleman, who treated us to a hearty refreshment before we entered the town. On entering, the bells rung a merry peal, and we had free entertainment as at Cambridge. There was a present of some money made here for our women, as well as for the men; that for the men was distributed; that for the women (of the second division) amounted to two pounds, and was handed over by Col. Dick** to Lieut. F., but this gentleman perhaps despised any ostentatious display of what he might have considered charity, and I never heard of its distribution.

Stilton, Stamford, and Grantham, welcomed us with the usual greetings; bells ringing merry peals, and the inhabitants cheering with joyful shouts as we approached their

---

* The regiment marched in two divisions, and that which the author accompanied was the second.
** Colonel Dick commanded the first division, which, of course, preceded the second by one day's stage; but he waited in Huntingdon until the latter marched in.

hospitable boundaries. At Newark we were not only received with the same demonstration of kindly welcoming and entertainment, but each man received a day's pay, being a gratuity from the magistrates. At Doncaster we were equally well received. Saturday being the day on which we entered, many of the respectable tradesmen met in the evening at the taverns, to spend a few hours at the social board, and they had the kindness to invite the soldiers billeted therein to enjoy the passing pleasures of the pot and pipe, song and conversation.

Pomfret was no less kind, while Wetherby and Boroughbridge, it may be said, excelled those towns which had shown the greatest liberality towards us; even our women were presented with an allowance of tea and sugar, and the soldiers with tobacco, for soldiers as well as sailors like the fragrant leaf. It was truly gratifying, on approaching one of those towns, to see the youth regimented and drawn up in their best holiday suits, with flags unfurled, and accompanied with music, welcoming us to their cheerful happy homes.

Northallerton and Darlington received us with every mark of esteem, and we entered Durham amidst the loud cheering of thousands and the merry peals of all the city bells. A donation equal to two days' pay was presented to each man, besides free entertainment in the respective houses in which we were quartered.

As we passed through the pleasant village of Houghton-le-Spring, we were halted and presented with an excellent refreshment. Congratulatory effusions from the pen of one of its generous sons appeared in print the following day, and were much admired by us in whose praise they were composed. From Houghton-le-Spring we continued our march to Sunderland, where the first division of the regiment had arrived the previous day. It being Sunday, a rather unusual day for troops marching in the time of peace, and in religious England too, an immense concourse of inhabitants met us on the way to welcome us to barracks.

We remained in Sunderland upwards of four weeks, during which time we were joined by the depot of the regiment from Scotland, and we again formed a pretty strong body.

On the 9th March we left Sunderland, where we had experienced much kindness, and proceeded on our route for Scotland.

Newcastle welcomed us in the same congratulatory manner as we had been received at Cambridge, Newark, and Durham. Morpeth, though a small town, was no less liberal in its manifestation of its good will towards us. I should be ungrateful not to record the kindness of Mr. Watson, one of its local magistrates or aldermen. With him I spent an agreeable evening, so far as he could make it so. It was his wish to hear and learn of Waterloo, and for this purpose he had personally invited the acting sergeant-major of the division (not the assistant sergeant-major before mentioned); but as this sergeant had not been with the regiment at Waterloo, Mr. W. requested him to invite one who had been there to accompany him. I was thus indebted to chance for the invitation. I am certain, however, that Mr. W. heard less of what he wanted to hear, than he did of that which he did not want to learn; for my more communicative neighbour engrossed the whole conversation, and I envied him not, for I suppose he had heard enough of Waterloo talk to make him peevish at hearing more about it.

Should this memoir ever reach the eye of Mr. Watson, I trust it will show to him that I remember his kindness with gratitude; may he live long to enjoy the fortune, which, by the blessing of Providence and his own exertions, he has been enabled to realize.

On entering Alnwick and receiving our billets, we were made acquainted that his grace the Duke of Northumberland had been pleased, through his agent, to order entertainment for each man in his respective quarters; and before we broke ranks, three hearty cheers were given as a "So be it," to the exclamation of "Long live the noble family of Percy!"

What recollections must not this manner of receiving us awaken in the minds of our border historians! When we look back to the days when England strove against Scotland, and Scotland against England; when the spear of the Percy was struck at the gate of the Douglas, and the sword of the Douglas was a firebrand at the threshold of the Percy. We now see the sons of the fathers' foes receive us with cordial welcome; and we, the children of the north, rejoice in the blessings which those of the south have taught us to appreciate.

We are now fast approaching our own blue bleak mountains; Belford is already behind, even Haggartston is in the rear; the lovely Tweed is in view; the cold hills of the north rise in the distance, while the snow falls thick around us.

England! we leave thee now behind; thou hast shown us too much kindness; if thy bounty and liberality has been in any instance abused, forgive our little knowledge of manners; for although our deportment may have been rude and apparently thankless, we nevertheless appreciate thy many acts of kindness bestowed upon us; not as upon mendicants, but as upon favourite children, and as such we have accepted and shall think of them with gratitude. If ever thou hast occasion for assistance to repel an invader or to attack a foe, call from those mountains the plaided sons of Caledonia, whom thy hospitality has taught to be grateful, and on whose hearts thy kindness has made a deep impression.

We rested two nights in Berwick, one in Ayton, and one in Dunbar; passed on for Haddington, but were halted at Linton, where we were treated in the same manner as we had been at Houghton-le-Spring.

We rested one night in Haddington and proceeded next day for Edinburgh, but were halted at the town-hall of Musselburgh, where a comfortable refreshment was placed before us, and to which ample justice was done. At Portobello an immense concourse of people were assembled to meet and welcome us. At Piershill the metropolis seemed to pour out the stream of its population to congratulate us on our approach, and to welcome us to its arms. Advance seemed impracticable, from the density of the surrounding multitude: from this a guard of cavalry, with its band of music, preceded us. Thus accompanied, we entered the city amidst the loud cheering and congratulatory acclamations of friends; while over our heads, from a thousand windows, waved as many banners, plaided scarfs, or other symbols of courtly greetings.

We entered the castle, proud of the most distinguished reception that ever a regiment had met with from a grateful country. Two nights we were admitted free to the Theatre, two to the Olympic Circus, two days to the panoramic view of Waterloo; and to conclude our triumphal rejoicings, after removing from the castle to Queensberry House Barracks, an entertainment was provided for us in the Assembly Rooms, George's Street, to which the noblemen and gentlemen contributors came, and witnessed the glee with which we enjoyed their hospitality. The drink was of the best, and fame tells a lie if the beer was not mixed with strong ale or spirits; and so plentifully was it supplied by active waiters during the dinner, that before the cloth was withdrawn we were very hearty. We enjoyed the glass till nearly sunset, by which time there was scarcely a man at the table but thought himself qualified to sing a song, make a speech, or give a toast, and not a few attempted to do the whole; and, if we had been allowed an hour's longer enjoyment, the heroes of Waterloo would have been prostrated under that table at which they had so lately sat in glorious glee, and all their laurels scattered in the dust.

We staggered out, bonnets falling off in all directions, got into our ranks, and marched off as if a whirlwind had been blowing amongst us and sweeping us out of our ranks. There lay one prostrate; another, attempting to raise him up, fell over him; while the loose folds of the kilt lapped upwards, and thus left his thighs un-curtained to the view of the numerous spectators who were looking down from the windows. Some ladies endeavoured to withdraw from the indelicate exhibition, but were so closely pent up by others, that they rendered themselves more prominent by their ineffectual struggles to retire.

We reached the North Bridge without leaving a man behind, but there we began to drop in couples, and although it was a calm pleasant afternoon, our heads were knocking against the balustrades of the bridge as if driven upon them by the violence of a tempest.

By the time our front files got to our barracks, the rear was broken, and groping or sprawling their way down the High Street. No lives were lost, though many a bonnet and kilt changed owners, and not a few disappeared entirely.

Brief as this account is, of the reception we met with, I make no doubt, but there are some who may think I have stated too much, particularly regarding our carousals; but to those who may think my observations uncalled for, I beg leave to say, they are just, and that I wish there had been less occasion for any remarks, for I have been extremely sparing in self-chastisement, and do not invite another to lift the rod. A candid confession from the lips of the guilty, ought to be more readily pardoned than when he is obliged by another to acknowledge his error.

Afterword

I feel myself called upon, before concluding, to offer some apologetic explanation regarding these memoirs; doubtless it would have been more appropriately placed as introductory matter in the first chapter, but I presume there is no great trespass in introducing it here.

From my entering the service in 1803, until 1811, I kept a journal of what I thought worthy of recording. This journal I composed in rhyme, and, to tell the truth, I thought it poetry. In 1811, I purchased a grammar, and after studying it a little, I was enabled to discover that I had trespassed against every rule of the art. And although there was nothing indelicate or offensive in my work, yet I was vexed that I had been so silly as to show it to men of learning, and committed it to the flames. Still I was bent on journalizing, and having once commenced in rhyme, I felt no inclination to discontinue; more particularly so, as my transfer of service to the line would doubtless enable me to witness events more worthy of record.

Having burned my former journal, I commenced my new one on my landing in Spain in 1813, and carried it on until 1816.

But what could be supposed to proceed from the pen of one who during his life had been almost a stranger to books, even to a dictionary? Useless in many respects as my efforts may be supposed to have been, yet they were not altogether so to myself. My scribbling vein was an amusement when on guard, and it was chiefly when I was on guard that I did write, as I found other exercise at other times; and I seldom lay down on the bench or the green turf to sleep, but sat writing and sometimes reading; the latter very seldom; but when I did, was pleased with the approval of those who were as little capable of judging of the merit of the work as I was myself.

In 1816 I ceased journalizing; with one duty or another, I found little time. I endeavoured, however, to correct what 1 had written, and was very proud to receive the flattering opinion of some of my superiors regarding the subject; and I must here confess, that two or three copies of this doggerel rhyme (which perhaps would have been considered not so bad in the days of the Edwards and the Braces, but was really contemptible for the age of the Georges) were put into the hands of a few whom I considered my friends.

In 1827 I had the pleasure of becoming acquainted with a gentleman who had an excellent library at his command, and by him was favoured with the perusal of some excellent books. I now began to see my rhyming journal, from 1813 to 1816, in almost the same contemptible light as I had done the preceding one which I had burned, and I set to remodel my manuscript. I therefore had only to transpose the subject of my rhyme to prose, and then question myself which of the two was the better.

I trust the reader will now perceive my reason for offering an apology. My rhyme journal, which my illiterate vanity made me think poetry, and from which I may say all but the first three chapters is a transposition, will partly account for some apostrophes which may be thought not altogether consistent with prose writing. If these in any respects violate the legitimate rules of composition and good taste, or approach to what some may call "prose run mad," I am to blame, and humbly apologize.

Having thus far brought my journal to a period of peace, and I may say, to the spot from which I set out for active service, I shall conclude.

Printed in the United Kingdom
by Lightning Source UK Ltd.
122803UK00002B/607-612/A